Managing
Your
Business
with

QUICKBOOKS 6

Charles Rubin & Diane Parssinen

Peachpit
Press

Managing Your Business with QuickBooks 6
Charles Rubin and Diane Parssinen

Peachpit Press
1249 Eighth Street
Berkeley, CA 94710
510/524-2178
510/524-2221 (fax)
800/283-9444

Find us on the World Wide Web at:
http://www.peachpit.com

Peachpit Press is a division of Addison Wesley Longman

Editor: Jeanne Woodward
Production Coordinator: Kate Reber
Copyeditor: Valerie Perry
Compositor: Melanie Haage
Indexer: Valerie Perry
Interior design: Mimi Heft
Cover design: TMA Ted Mader Associates, Inc.

ISBN: 0-201-35356-3
9 8 7 6 5 4 3 2 1

Printed and bound in the United States

Dedication

To Ed, for hanging in there. Again.
—Diane Parssinen

To Jim Ellson, Bob Greer, and Sal Romo, three great accountants
who deserve clients as well organized as QuickBooks can make them.
—Charles Rubin

Acknowledgments

We'd like to offer a very big thanks to Dru Gregory of Intuit, who cheerfully answered a lot of questions, provided prerelease software and extensive documentation as promised, and generally personified the ease of use and convenience for which all of Intuit's products are justly renowned. Every company should have such people.

We are also grateful to the extremely pleasant and productive employees and contractors of Peachpit Press, including Jeanne Woodward, our project editor; Valerie Perry, our manuscript editor; Mimi Heft, the creator of a great interior design; and Kate Reber, the production coordinator. No author makes books without people like these and we are very fortunate to have worked with these people in particular.

—Charles Rubin and Diane Parssinen

TABLE OF CONTENTS

Part II: Running Your Business with Quickbooks 109

INTRODUCTION

There are dozens of accounting programs for Windows. In just a few years, however, QuickBooks has captured about 80 percent of the accounting market for companies with one to 20 employees. QuickBooks has become a smash hit because it handles small business accounting chores in the simplest possible way. Of course, the "simplest possible way" is still pretty complicated if you're a small business owner with little training in accounting and very little time to learn about it. Even if you're painfully aware that your business needs a computerized accounting system—and even if you already own QuickBooks—you may be unable to get started with it. It may seem like a complex process and you can't ever find the spare time you need to get it up and running.

 Note: *Throughout this book, we use "QuickBooks" to refer to both QuickBooks 6 and QuickBooks Pro 6 unless we specifically mention a difference.*

Right now, in fact, you may be within an arm's reach of a nicely shrink-wrapped QuickBooks package that you intended to install but never quite did. Or you may be sitting in front of a QuickBooks system on your PC that you installed weeks or months ago, but you have given up hope of understanding the program well enough for it to help you in your business. You may even have bought other books about QuickBooks in the hope that they would help you get a handle on what seems to be a monumental task, but you still haven't been able to make the transition from paper to computerized bookkeeping.

We wrote this book because you're not alone. Thousands of people with all kinds of businesses are in the same position as you. Between answering phones, managing employees, serving customers, and possibly raising a family, it's tough to find the time to get going with QuickBooks.

Maybe you don't understand accounting systems well enough to be able to convert your system to QuickBooks or any other full-fledged accounting program. Perhaps your accountant or bookkeeper does the heavy record keeping for you and you know very little about the process.

And even if you understand your present accounting system, you may despair of ever understanding QuickBooks well enough to adapt it to your own business. After all, different accounting systems and programs use different names for common accounting functions.

Or, finally, it may be that the whole idea of putting in a new accounting system seems incredibly complex, time-consuming, and just plain scary. You don't want to risk giving up your current accounting system—no matter how inefficient it might be—because you can't quite be sure that you'll understand the new one as well or that it will do everything it promises.

Why You Need This Book

If you have any or all of the above problems, this book is for you. Unlike other books about QuickBooks, this one is short and readable. It breaks up the process of switching to and using QuickBooks into manageable chunks. It explains computer-based accounting in terms you can relate to your own business, and it shows you how to budget time for each step of the process so you can make an orderly transition to a vastly superior accounting system. Here's how we do it:

In Chapter 1, we explain how to get up and running with QuickBooks. You'll learn how to start the program, and how to use its menus, buttons, forms, dialog boxes, and Help system.

In Chapter 2, we explain the basic elements of business accounting, using the same terms QuickBooks uses so you can relate them to the program right away.

In Chapter 3, we show you how to map out a strategy for converting from your current accounting system to QuickBooks. You'll learn how to budget your time for a QuickBooks conversion, how to organize your current records so they'll be easy to enter into QuickBooks, and how the whole process will proceed. This takes the fear and uncertainty out of making the switch.

In Chapter 4, we'll show you how to set up QuickBooks to accurately capture and reflect the financial activity of your particular business.

In Chapter 5, you'll find out how to customize QuickBooks by setting preferences, customizing forms and using templates, setting up users and passwords, and how to get free updates to the program from the Internet.

In Chapters 6, 7, 9, and 10, we go through typical daily, weekly, monthly, quarterly, and tax-time accounting tasks as you will do them in QuickBooks. We'll show you the basics of the main activities you'll perform, then refer you to specific sections of the QuickBooks online Help system and manual for more details.

Chapter 8 shows you how to get "snapshots" of your business activity with reports and graphs.

Finally, we include two Appendixes. Appendix A explains how Quick-Books works in multiuser environments and points you to sections of the book that discuss specific multiuser operations. Appendix B shows you how to customize your QuickBooks setup for twenty different types of businesses. There's also a glossary of terms for your reference.

Essentially, this book will take you from your present accounting system to a QuickBooks system that makes your record keeping easier and more effective than ever before. You'll be able to print payroll checks in a few minutes each week, produce sales and cash flow reports, and come up with everything you need to pay taxes much more quickly than you ever could before.

Why Computerize Your Accounting with QuickBooks?

Accurate bookkeeping is the life-support system of every business. And if you want the most accurate, flexible, and up-to-date way to maintain your business records, a computerized accounting system is the only way to go. Because your computer can easily organize and retrieve data, a computer-based accounting program is a precise indicator of the health of your business at any point in time. A good computerized accounting system gives you the information you need as you need it, so you can do the following:

- Quickly make decisions about what products or services to offer and how to price them.

- See how changes in your business have affected employee productivity.

- Find out how much you'll owe in payroll taxes each week or month.

- Produce up-to-the-minute financial reports for creating a business plan or obtaining a bank loan.

Accounting language and procedures often seem technical and confusing. QuickBooks does a sophisticated job of accounting, but mercifully, it keeps most of the technical and confusing operations in the background so you don't have to worry about them. Based on the same philosophy as Quicken —the personal accounting program that has organized millions—Quick-Books uses simple forms to collect information. All the tasks you need to perform are handled by filling in these forms and QuickBooks does the complicated accounting work in the background.

QuickBooks makes your accounting life easier in several important areas. A few of these are described below.

Record Keeping

If you've tried keeping accurate records with a paper system, you know it's a time-consuming and repetitive process because you have to enter the same information on many different pieces of paper. If you sell an item, you generate a sales record. At the end of the day, you add all the sales totals to a daily sales report, then fill out a deposit slip for your bank. And when tax time comes, you have to go through dozens of daily sales reports to figure out your taxes. The whole process is loaded with opportunities for error as you transcribe and manually calculate numbers. With QuickBooks, though, you enter sales, expense, and employee payroll information only once. Every piece of data you enter becomes available for use in many forms— including invoices, sales reports, payroll checks, and tax reports.

When you have a manual record-keeping system, you have to hunt down several pieces of paper (individual receipts or invoices, for example) in order to determine your cash flow or project future expenses. This is such a hassle that you probably avoid it at all costs unless you're forced by your banker, accountant, or the IRS. But when you use QuickBooks, getting reports is easy. You can generate reports to give detailed balance sheets, profit and loss statements, accounts receivable or sales reports, inventory reports, accounts payable reports, budgets, payroll reports, project cost analyses, cash flow forecasts, mailing lists, and even a check register. Any QuickBooks report can be easily customized to show only information from specific time intervals, specific salespeople, specific customers, or other details, so you have great flexibility in the number of ways you can view information about the state of your business.

Simpler, Faster Data Entry

Most computerized accounting systems can record information and produce reports, but QuickBooks is the easiest accounting program to use because it incorporates a lot of smart features. For example, QuickBooks memorizes transactions so that once they are entered, they may be reentered with just a few keystrokes. If you write a check to Big Dog Linen Service every month, you can type just a few letters of the company's name and QuickBooks will automatically fill in the date, the amount of the check, and the vendor's address. At the same time, QuickBooks will also reduce your checking account balance by the amount of the check, then add the same amount to the expense account you have set up for laundry. You can even group sets of recurring transactions to do them all at once at predetermined intervals. For example, you might pay all your utility and building maintenance bills on the same day every month. You can also use online banking and payroll services to further automate these processes.

Financing

Inadequate financing is one of the most common reasons that small businesses fail. And it's often hard for a business to obtain adequate financing simply because the owner can't present a comprehensive statement of financial health to a bank. QuickBooks allows instant and accurate reporting in the standard format requested by most lending institutions. It also produces ongoing reports that may be required by lenders, such as accounts receivable or sales tax statements.

Because QuickBooks keeps all your company's data in memory, it's easy to see your expected income, expenses, and bank account balances at a glance. You can forecast exactly how much cash you'll have in order to plan future purchasing, ad campaigns, hiring, or expansion. This information also helps when you write your business plan for bankers or potential investors.

Payroll

Hiring employees and keeping track of hours, salaries and wages, social security numbers and dependents, vacation and sick time, bonuses and advances, and company contributions to government and private pension plans can be a nightmare in itself. Many businesses farm out their payroll operations to a bookkeeper so they don't have to deal with it all. With Quick-Books, you can handle your payroll quickly and easily. When you hire an employee, you simply enter the personal and salary information into an employee record. Keeping track of an employee's time and allocating it to different customers or jobs is just as easy.

When it comes time to produce your payroll, you simply choose which employees you want to pay. QuickBooks remembers how many hours have been worked, calculates gross wages, deducts taxes, figures employer contributions, and prepares the check. In QuickBooks version 6, you can even send your payroll data to an online payroll service and have the service create checks and make direct deposits for you with guaranteed accuracy.

Taxes

Federal, state, and local taxes are also a challenge for any small business owner. Not only do you have to keep accurate records of all your expenses and income, but you also have to report the results accurately and on time to avoid penalties and excess tax paid. Payroll taxes can be especially daunting, with different tax percentages, withholding, and employer contributions for each employee. Sales taxes add their own headaches in terms of collecting, tracking, and reporting—sometimes to several different agencies.

QuickBooks automatically figures out employee withholding and employer contributions. Once you enter each employee's withholding information, QuickBooks uses built-in tax tables to determine all federal and state taxes, plus withholding and employer contributions. As the tax laws change, you can easily update these tables online so you're always reporting the right figures. QuickBooks keeps track of data you need to produce quarterly 941 reports and payments. It also figures W-2s, W-3s, and 1099s and prints them at year's end.

When you create invoices that include taxable items, QuickBooks can automatically calculate and include sales taxes. These taxes are then tracked according to the time when sales taxes are payable to the tax agencies. So, for example, if you pay monthly sales taxes, you can quickly produce a monthly report showing how much you owe, whom you owe it to, and when it is due.

A Simplified Accounting System

Any accounting program can get you organized, but QuickBooks makes it easy. It integrates all aspects of small business accounting so you can do everything with just one program. When you install QuickBooks and set it up for your company, the program asks you questions about your business and then tailors itself to your specific requirements.

When you need to enter data, QuickBooks uses onscreen forms that look just like the paper forms you use every day, such as checks, account registers, invoices, purchase orders, and time cards. Once you fill in these forms, QuickBooks handles the accounting invisibly in the background so the information is correct and available whenever you need to make a report.

QuickBooks keeps track of your business data with lists. These lists organize vital business information and make it available for a variety of accounting needs. For example, one list is a chart of accounts that shows all your expense categories. Another is a list of items you sell. Others contain the names of customers or jobs, vendors, or employees. All lists have information windows that make it easy for you to enter or update your information.

QuickBooks keeps a register for each of your accounts so you can see a list of transactions in that account, organized by date. For example, you can select a customer name and see every invoice sent to or paid by that customer.

Finally, unlike many other accounting programs, QuickBooks is very forgiving. If you make a mistake entering an invoice total or payroll amount, you can simply correct it. (In other programs, you correct mistakes by making new entries to offset the original ones, which translates into twice as much work.) And while you can easily change information you store with QuickBooks, you can also protect your data with passwords so nobody can look at or change anything without your permission.

What's New in QuickBooks 6

As usual, the folks at Intuit have been working tirelessly to improve Quick-Books. Unlike other software firms we could name, Intuit actually listens to its customer suggestions when upgrading its programs. In fact, QuickBooks now includes hyperlinks you can click to provide feedback directly to Intuit via the Internet.

Here are some of the ways that QuickBooks and QuickBooks Pro have been improved in version 6.

Ease of Use

QuickBooks has built a reputation for being easy to use, so it's not surprising that the latest version includes new features that improve its convenience and simplicity.

- New How Do I? buttons on many screen forms give you quick access to a series of Help system topics that explain specific procedures for that form. Among the topics, you'll find Show Me videos, which are multimedia presentations about key QuickBooks procedures.

- A new Payroll Item Setup wizard walks you through the options when you create or change payroll items.

- Right-mouse menus appear on transaction forms when you click the right mouse button, giving you faster access to key program actions associated with each form.

- A User Setup wizard that helps you create user names and passwords and decide which privileges to grant each new user.

Better Internet Resources and Access

The Internet and World Wide Web have become much more important as means of communication and information access, and Intuit is right in step with this trend. Intuit has had one of the most helpful small business Web sites for the past few years, and the site has been expanded with more articles about small business management, better online technical support, and online banking, payroll, and tax table update services. QuickBooks 6 has a fully integrated Web browser that makes it easier to access those Web resources and then return to other QuickBooks activities. If you don't have a Web browser, you can install one from the QuickBooks CD-ROM.

If you sign up for Intuit's new payroll and direct deposit services (which carry a monthly fee), you can transmit payroll information to Intuit's Web site and Intuit will prepare paychecks and even deposit them to the bank accounts of your employees with guaranteed accuracy.

Multiuser Capability in QuickBooks Pro

Many small business owners asked for a program that more than one employee could use at a time, and Intuit responded by adding multiuser capabilities to QuickBooks Pro version 6. With QuickBooks Pro 6, up to five users can access and view data at the same time.

Quicken, QuickBooks, and QuickBooks Pro

There are many different programs for bookkeeping, but QuickBooks and QuickBooks Pro are the recognized leaders. Basically, QuickBooks Pro has come along because QuickBooks doesn't handle service companies well. Also, many people now using QuickBooks may have upgraded from Quicken when they started their own businesses. Here's an overview of the major differences between these three programs.

Quicken

Years before QuickBooks and QuickBooks Pro appeared, many small businesses began using Quicken because it was much simpler than other accounting packages. You can use Quicken to track multiple income and expense accounts, but it requires a separate program (QuickPay) to handle payroll, and it makes managing a normal business more difficult. For example, it doesn't track bills payable or manage inventory and it won't allow you to make estimates or write invoices. You can't group items (such as vendors or income sources) into classes as you can with QuickBooks and QuickBooks Pro.

QuickBooks

QuickBooks gives you much more flexibility for tracking your business activities, and it allows you to include much more detail about your transactions. You can group expenses into classes and then track income and expenses by class. For example, if you own 10 hot dog stands around a tourist attraction, you create a class for each stand so you can track expenses and revenues by stand. This way, you'll know where to place the stands for better sales and when to fire the operators for eating up your profits.

QuickBooks also handles payroll chores. It prints paychecks, tracks payroll taxes and employer contributions, and includes several payroll-oriented reports. In version 6, you can even transmit your payroll to Intuit for paycheck processing and direct deposits.

At the end of the year, QuickBooks will automatically produce 1099s for consultants you hire. It will walk you through the process of filling out W-2s, and it will print them along with the W-3 cover sheet; handling 941 forms is equally simple.

QuickBooks is better for businesses that sell goods rather than services because it doesn't handle time tracking and it has no built-in features for job cost analysis.

QuickBooks Pro

If you like the simplicity of QuickBooks but want a multiuser program that can support several different users on a company network, QuickBooks Pro is for you. Even if you don't need multiuser capability, QuickBooks Pro is the program to choose if you are an accountant, lawyer, consultant, construction contractor, or someone else who charges for his or her time. The included QuickBooks Pro Timer program allows you to keep track of time worked on each job and makes it easy to bill time to the correct client. QuickBooks Pro can also store time data in weekly timecards, and it can assign hours worked to each job so you can bill clients accordingly.

Whether you choose QuickBooks or QuickBooks Pro for your business, this book will help you get up and running as painlessly as possible.

Where to Go from Here

This book is divided into two parts. The first five chapters introduce Quick-Books and basic accounting concepts and terms, and they show you how to organize your records and set up QuickBooks for your business. We suggest you read these chapters in order, then follow their instructions as soon as your time permits.

If you have trouble setting up QuickBooks for your business, check the customization templates in Appendix B, "Customizing QuickBooks for Your Business," for help. If you're uncertain about QuickBooks Pro's multiuser operations, check out Appendix A, "Multiuser Features in QuickBooks Pro," for a quick overview. And if you run across a term you don't understand, look for it in the Glossary.

The second part of the book covers periodic accounting activities. For now, concentrate on Chapter 6, "Daily Activities," and Chapter 7, "Weekly and Monthly Activities," so you can begin performing the daily and weekly tasks you'll need to record your accounting information into QuickBooks. Chapter 8 shows you how to produce the various types of reports you'll need for your business. Read Chapter 9, "Quarterly Activities," and Chapter 10, "Year-end and Tax-Time Activities," when you reach the end of the first quarter, year, or tax-reporting period under your new QuickBooks system.

How We Present Information

Our goal is to give you the essential information you need to get up and running with QuickBooks as quickly as possible, not to provide an exhaustive reference about the program (we think the online Help and documentation handle that job pretty well.) As a result, we won't cover every menu command or every option on every screen. If you have a question about a program feature we don't cover, you'll find an explanation in the online Help system, which we cover in Chapter 1, "Working with QuickBooks."

Here are some other notes on this book's format:

- We capitalize the names of all commands, menus, and dialog box options for reading ease; many names that contain multiple words are not capitalized in the program itself.

- We specify menu commands with the menu name, a right angle bracket, and the command name. For example, when we say, "Choose File > Open Company," we mean for you to choose the Open Company command from the File menu.

- We specify submenu commands like this: "Choose Reports > Profit & Loss > Standard," which means to choose the Standard command from the Profit & Loss submenu on the Reports menu.

- We don't include ellipses at the end of command names that have them (we say "Open Company," not "Open Company…")

- When we tell you to select a radio button or checkbox option, we tell you to "select" or "click" the button or "check" the checkbox to put a selection dot or checkmark in it. When we want you to deselect one of these options, we tell you to "deselect" a button or "uncheck" a checkbox to remove the selection dot or checkmark.

- When we tell you to "click" with the mouse, we always mean for you to use the left mouse button unless we say otherwise.

- We specify data to enter by using bold text. For example, we say: type **Joe's Bar** in the Name box.

What You Need to Begin

This book is about QuickBooks, not Microsoft Windows. Before you begin you should be familiar with the basic Windows interface, such as choosing commands from menus; opening, closing, scrolling, and resizing windows; and selecting things with the mouse. You'll also need to understand words like "taskbar," "menu bar," "icon," "dialog box," and "scroll bar." If you have trouble with any of these operations or concepts, we suggest you choose Help from the Start menu in the lower-left corner of your screen to learn them.

Taking the Plunge

Setting up a new accounting system is a scary thing, but by following the instructions in this book, you'll be able to focus on and handle one step of the process at a time. Before you know it, you'll be creating up-to-the-minute reports on payables, receivables, or payroll costs, or impressing your accountant with a neat, orderly statement of your business activity for the year. QuickBooks has the potential to give you more control over your business facts than you ever thought possible. You can begin realizing that potential by turning the page.

PART I

SETTING UP QUICKBOOKS

WORKING WITH QUICKBOOKS

In this chapter, you'll find out how to use the QuickBooks commands, buttons, screen forms, and Help system. We'll assume that you've already installed QuickBooks following the Getting Started guide in the QuickBooks package.

Starting and Exploring QuickBooks

The changes in QuickBooks over the years have made it easier to use and more powerful. Each time you run QuickBooks, you'll find an array of Help facilities and several different ways to choose commands.

Once your software is installed, double-click the QuickBooks icon on your desktop or choose Programs > QuickBooks > QuickBooks from the Start menu at the lower-left corner of your Windows screen. You'll see the startup dialog box shown in Figure 1.1.

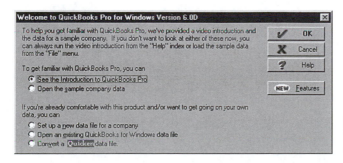

Figure 1.1
The Startup options
dialog box.

As you can see, there are lots of ways to explore QuickBooks. You can look at a multimedia introduction, check out a sample data file, see what's new in the latest version of QuickBooks, or view the program's Help file.

Viewing the QuickBooks Files

If you're new to QuickBooks, we recommend choosing the Welcome to QuickBooks option first. You'll see a collection of short video files that introduce key concepts about the program. Each video takes just a couple of minutes to watch, and you can stop the presentation whenever you want. Spend some time with these videos; they will make you more comfortable with the program when you begin using it on your own.

 Note: *You'll need to install the QuickBooks CD-ROM to run the Introduction to QuickBooks videos, and you'll need a sound card and speakers to hear the narration that goes with them.*

If you're upgrading your copy of QuickBooks to the latest version, click the New Features 6.0 button. You'll see a list of the new features in this version of the program. Scroll down the window to read about all the new features.

Exploring the Sample Data File

The next thing you'll want to do in your orientation is to see what a QuickBooks data file looks like. QuickBooks comes with a sample file containing data from a fictional construction company. To open this file, click the Open The Sample Company Data button in the Startup dialog box and then click the OK button.

 Note: *If the Startup dialog box isn't showing anymore, choose File > Open Company, and then open the file named "sample" in the dialog box that appears.*

Managing Windows and the QuickBooks Navigator

When you open the sample company file, you'll see the QuickBooks Navigator window, the Reminders list window, and a QCard description of the Reminders list. These components are all shown in Figure 1.2.

Figure 1.2 The sample company file opens with the Navigator window, the Reminders list, and a visible Qcard.

You can use either the Navigator or the menus at the top of the screen to control QuickBooks. QCards are brief messages that describe what you see on the screen.

 Tip: *You can close any QCard window by clicking its close box. To turn off QCards completely, see "Hiding and Showing QCards" later in this chapter under "Getting Help."*

Each time you open a list of items (reminders, accounts, vendors or customers, for example) or perform an activity (such as writing a check or creating an invoice), you open a new window. Each window appears in its own invisible layer, so you can move one window on top of another by dragging it. You can have as many windows open on the screen as your computer's available memory allows, but it's best to put each window away when you're done with it.

Activating a Window

You may have lots of different windows open on your screen, but only one of them can be active at a time. The active window is always in the top layer on your screen, so it covers up anything directly behind it. You must activate a window in order to drag it around the screen, resize it, use its features, or close it. You can tell which window is active because its title and scroll bars are displayed normally and its name is selected with a checkmark on the Window menu. An inactive form has grayed-out title and scroll bars. To activate a window, click anywhere in it or choose its name from the Window menu.

Closing or Hiding a Window

You can use the close, minimize, and maximize buttons at the top-right corner of any window to close or resize it. But you don't have to close a window to hide it from view. If a window is small like the Reminders window in Figure 1.2, simply activating a larger window underneath it will bring that window forward, hiding the smaller one.

Using the QuickBooks Navigator

The QuickBooks Navigator window breaks up the QuickBooks operations into functional areas, so you can find and use a particular feature by relating it to a part of your accounting process. To see how this works, activate the Navigator window by clicking in it. The Navigator window (shown in Figure 1.3) moves to the top.

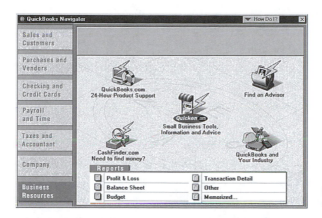

Figure 1.3 The Navigator window.

When you click a tab at the left, the rest of the Navigator window changes. (In Figure 1.3, the Business Resources tab is clicked.) The center

GIVE QUICKBOOKS ENOUGH MEMORY

When QuickBooks runs low on available memory, some rather nasty things occur, such as the check order or balances going haywire in your checking account register. To keep this from happening, close each form as soon as you're finished with it. You can open as many forms at a time as your computer's memory allows, but it's a good idea to keep open only the forms you need to work with at any given time.

Another way you can cut down on how much memory QuickBooks uses is by telling it not to save the desktop. Normally, QuickBooks remembers every form or window you have open when you quit the program, and it opens them all up again the next time you start up. This saves time if you use particular forms or windows regularly, but it also uses extra memory. To turn off this feature:

1. *Choose File > Preferences to open the Preferences dialog box.*

2. *Click the General icon at the left side of the Preferences dialog box.*

3. *Click the Don't Save The Desktop button.*

4. *Click the OK button to save the change and put the dialog box away.*

For more information about preferences, see "Setting QuickBooks Preferences" in Chapter 5.

of the screen usually shows a flow diagram with different accounting activities such as making sales, buying goods, or paying employees. Click any of the icons in the flow chart and you'll open a QuickBooks form that supports that part of the process, such as an invoice or purchase order form.

At the top of the Navigator window is a row of icons you can click to display lists of information about customers, vendors, employees, and other data.

The bottom of the Navigator window offers a list of reports that pertain to the functional area of the program that you're working in.

Try clicking the various tabs and icons to see how they navigate you to different QuickBooks features quickly and easily. In most cases, you'll see data on customers, inventory, invoices, employees, and other items for the sample company file.

Before continuing, click the QB Navigator button in the menu bar to bring the Navigator to the top again.

Using Forms

Whenever you record transactions, add or change customers or vendors, pay employees, or perform other operations to work with data in QuickBooks, you use a form. The forms you fill in for these activities have many features in common and are easy to understand. We'll explain how to use QuickBooks forms here. When we refer to various forms and activities later, we'll assume you know the basic mechanics of using a form—just refer back to this section if you have any questions.

Opening a Form

A form appears when you perform an activity that requires you to specify a lot of data. Such activities might include writing a check, making a deposit, creating an invoice, or changing the information you've stored about a vendor, item, or employee. To see how this works:

1. Click the Sales and Customers tab at the left side of the Navigator window.

2. Click the Receive Payments icon in the flow chart at the right. The Receive Payments form appears, as shown in Figure 1.4.

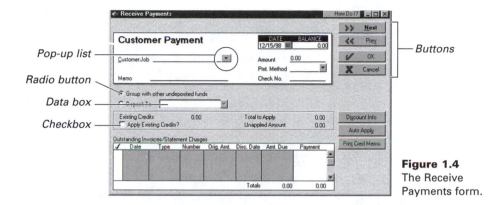

Pop-up list

Radio button

Data box

Checkbox

Buttons

Figure 1.4
The Receive
Payments form.

Each form is identified by a unique name—Receive Payments, Write Checks, or Create Invoices, for example—in its title bar. Forms contain the following elements:

- **Data boxes.** Type your data after the blinking cursor in the active data box. Press the Tab key to move through the form from one box to the next or press Shift-Tab to move backwards. (See the sidebar "How QuickBooks Helps You Enter Data" later in this chapter for more information.)

- **Radio buttons or checkboxes.** Click a radio button or checkbox to select its option and place a dot or checkmark in it; click it again to remove the dot or checkmark and deselect the option.

- **Pop-up lists.** Click on the pop-up list triangle button to display a list of choices, and then drag down the list to select the option you want. That option will be entered in the adjacent data blank.

- **Menu buttons.** Click on and hold open a menu button to display a menu or lists of options. When a menu button is next to a data box, select an item from the list or menu to enter it in that box.

- **Buttons.** Click a button to tell QuickBooks what to do with the entire form, get advice about using the form, or access other information.

  - **OK** saves the data you've entered and puts the form away.

  - **Next** saves the data you've entered and displays a new, blank form (this is handy when you're adding several new customer or vendor records, for example).

- **Prev** (or Previous) saves the data you've entered and displays the previous form you filled in.

- **Cancel** puts the form away without saving any data in it.

- **How Do I?** Clicking this button displays a menu of Help topics that explain how to perform various operations related to the current form.

Tip: *You can customize any QuickBooks form, adding or removing fields from it, changing the format of the form, or changing which information is shown when the form is printed. See Chapter 5, "Customizing and Updating QuickBooks," for more information.*

Depending on the form you're filling in, there may also be buttons you can click to print the form, to view data from another part of QuickBooks, to change the appearance of the form, or to set other options.

Finally, some forms have a set of tabs like the ones shown in Figure 1.5.

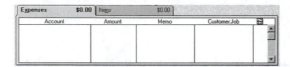

Figure 1.5 Tabs in some forms allow you to enter data for different types of transactions, such as income or expenses.

You'll find tabs above the detail area in checks, bill entry forms, or employee information forms, among others. Clicking one tab or another displays a different set of data blanks. For example, a check's detail area has tabs to display information blanks for items or expenses.

Tip: *The fastest way to get help in filling out a form is to display the form and then click the How Do I? button. You'll see a menu of options for learning about different aspects of the accounting process handled by that form. Just choose the option for which you want to display help.*

HOW QUICKBOOKS HELPS YOU ENTER DATA

On QuickBooks forms, data boxes that should contain information you may already have stored in QuickBooks (such as vendor names, item names, or employee names) feature a pop-up list, indicated with a Triangle button. For example, if you're working in the Item box of an invoice, you'll see a pop-up list with the names of all the items you've stored in QuickBooks, so you can simply choose the one you want instead of typing it.

QuickBooks also has a "clairvoyance" feature. When you type the first few letters of a vendor, employee, customer, or item name, the program guesses the rest of it and fills it in. If the name is the one you want, press the Tab key to move to the next data box or click in a different part of the form. If the suggested name isn't the one you want, continue typing to complete the entry.

If a data box contains a date, there's a miniature Calendar icon next to it. Rather than typing the date, you can click the Calendar icon to display a one-month calendar for the current month, and then click the date you want in that calendar. You can also click arrows next to the calendar's month name to display other months. Another way to change the date without typing it is to select the date and then press the + (plus) or - (minus) key on your keyboard; the date will increase or decrease a day at a time.

Finally, any numeric-data blank can be used as a miniature adding machine. If you type a number in the dollar-amount blank on a check, for example, and then enter a numeric operator (+, -, *, or /), a little tally tape appears. You can then add, subtract, multiply or divide a series of numbers. As you add numbers to the calculation, they appear on the tape. Once you have completed your calculation formula, press the Enter key and the total will be entered in the data blank.

Practicing with Forms

To practice using forms on your own, click any of the Flow Chart icons in the Navigator window to see various forms, or choose an accounting activity from the Activities menu (see below). Experiment by filling in some sample data of your own. You can always put a form away without saving your changes by clicking its close box or the Cancel button, and you can store a new transaction by clicking the OK button. (In some cases, you'll notice that QuickBooks won't let you click OK to store a transaction if you haven't filled in some required data boxes on the form, such as customer or vendor names.)

By simply fooling around with the commands and playing with the sample data, you'll get an understanding of the look and feel of a QuickBooks company and how to enter your data. Don't be afraid to try everything out. The sample data is there for you to play with—you can't hurt anything.

Using Lists

Another type of window you'll use frequently is a list. Choose Lists > Chart of Accounts to see a list of accounts (accounting categories) that have been set up for the sample company. This will give you an idea of how to set up accounts for your own firm. Figure 1.6 displays a Chart of Accounts list.

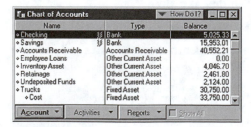

Figure 1.6 The Chart of Accounts list shows your expense and income categories.

Lists show the names of accounts, reminders, customers, employees, vendors, or some transactions such as purchase orders. To view the detailed information about a list item, just double-click it.

You can also select a list item and then perform other operations with it by using the menu buttons at the bottom of the list window. (See "Menu buttons," later in this chapter.)

Using Registers

A third kind of window you'll use frequently in QuickBooks is an account register. Like the register in your checkbook, registers show the details of individual transactions. You can always view an individual transaction form, but a register shows you all the transactions for an account. You can sort transactions in a register by date, amount, or other criteria, and you can also use a register to quickly enter new transactions or edit existing ones.

Viewing a Register

To view a register:

1. Open the Chart of Accounts list if it's not still open on your screen.

2. Double-click the account whose register you want to see. You'll see the register window shown in Figure 1.7.

Figure 1.7 A register window for a checking account.

 Tip: *You can also select an account name and press Ctrl-R to open the register, or choose Use Register with the Activities menu button. Transactions are normally listed in chronological order and each transaction normally occupies two lines.*

3. To display transactions on one line, check the One-line check box at the bottom of the register.

4. To sort transactions differently, choose an option from the Sort By pop-up list at the lower-right corner of the window.

Entering Data into a Register

To enter a new transaction:

1. Click anywhere in the bottom row of the register. The date will be selected so you can enter a different one if you want.

2. Type a new date (or use the Calendar icon, as explained under "Using Forms,"earlier in this chapter), and then press the Tab key to move to the Number column.

3. Enter a transaction or check number and then press Tab to move to the Payee column.

4. Continue entering data (using pop-up lists or typing) until the transaction data is complete.

5. Click the Record button to store the new transaction. The ending register balance in the lower-right corner of the register is automatically updated.

You can use the other buttons at the bottom of the register to perform these additional tasks:

- To cancel any changes you've made, click the Restore button.

- To edit the transaction using the actual transaction form, click the Edit button.

- To add details of split transactions, click the Splits button (see "Splitting Transactions" in Chapter 6).

- To display the register's data in a report, click the Q-Report button (see "Using QuickReports" at the beginning of Chapter 8).

- To find a particular transaction based on accounts or names in the register, click the Go To button (see "Finding Transactions" in Chapter 6).

Using Menus and Menu Buttons

The QuickBooks Navigator is especially useful when you're new to the program, but once you know what you want, you may find it faster to choose QuickBooks features from menus. Just select a command from a menu or submenu at the top of the screen to perform an operation or display a form, list, or report.

 Note: *Most of the commands on the Online menu require you to have a modem and telephone line connected to your computer. See "Using Online Features in QuickBooks" later in this chapter.*

Right-mouse Menus

Whenever you're working in a form, list, or register, you can display a pop-up menu of commands specific to that window. QuickBooks uses right-mouse menus to put the commands you need most in the handiest possible location. To display a right-mouse menu, point to any part of the form, list, or register window, and click the right mouse button. A right-mouse menu will appear, like the one shown in Figure 1.8.

Figure 1.8 The right-mouse menu for the Create Invoices form.

This menu lets you perform a variety of activities that are related to the form you're using at the time. Since the right-mouse menu in Figure 1.8 is from the Create Invoices form, it has commands such as Find, for locating other invoices, and QuickReport, for making a report of all invoice transactions.

Menu Buttons

QuickBooks uses menu buttons in list windows as another way to place appropriate commands closer to the action. For example, the Account, Activities, and Reports buttons appear at the bottom of the Chart of Accounts list shown in Figure 1.6 (page 26). Note that the Activities and Reports menu buttons have the same names as two of the main program menus. The difference is that the menu button menus in this window contain only commands related specifically to items in the Chart of Accounts list, while the main menus contain commands for all parts of the program. To see the difference, click the Activities menu button to see its list of commands and then open the Activities menu at the top of the screen.

 Note: *We like menu buttons, but for the sake of clarity in this book, we typically refer you to the menus at the top of the screen. When we want you to use a menu button, we'll suggest it.*

One menu button in a list window lets you perform housekeeping chores with the list, such as adding, deleting, or renaming items. In the example above, the Account button lets you do this.

Exploring Other Menus

Feel free to open any of the menus and choose their commands. You'll see a form, list, or dialog box, and you'll quickly get an idea of how things work in QuickBooks. For example, open the Activities menu and take a quick look at the various activities listed there. Many of these have their own icons in the QuickBooks Navigator. You might also want to choose different reports from the Reports menu.

 Tip: *The Lists and Activities menus contain lots of choices. You can simplify them by moving infrequently used commands to the Other Lists and Other Activities submenus. To do this, choose File > Preferences, select Menus in the list of icons at the left side of the dialog box, and then click the checkboxes for the commands you want to move.*

Using the Iconbar

As if the menus, menu buttons, and the Navigator weren't enough, you can also use the Iconbar to open forms or perform other actions in QuickBooks. To display the Iconbar:

1. Choose File > Preferences to display the Preferences dialog box.

2. Click the Iconbar option in the scrolling list at the left of the Preferences dialog box.

3. Click one of the options at the right to display the Iconbar.

4. Click the OK button. You'll see a row of icons beneath the menu bar on the screen, like the one shown in Figure 1.9.

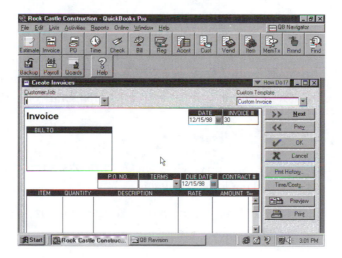

Figure 1.9 The Iconbar lets you perform QuickBooks operations by clicking icons.

 Note: *You can also use the Preferences dialog box to customize the Iconbar by adding or removing icons from it. For more information, choose Iconbar in the Preferences dialog box and then click the Help button.*

With the Iconbar in view, you can perform activities by simply clicking the appropriate icon.

Getting Help

QuickBooks provides several different types of help, from instructions on performing specific tasks to advice about using the program for your particular business. There are also many different ways to access help, depending on which screen or form you're viewing at the time. You can:

- Choose one of the commands on the Help menu at any time.

- Click the How Do I? button in forms or lists to see a menu of topics about specific procedures related to the active window.

- Click the Help button in a dialog box, press the F1 key, or choose Help On This Window to get an overview of the form, list, or dialog box you're using.

- Choose the Help command from the right-mouse menu on a form or register. You'll see an overview of the form or register you're using. (See "Right-mouse Menus" earlier in this chapter.)

We'll look at the Help window itself first, and then we'll see what other kinds of information you get with the Help menu commands.

The Help Window

Most of the assistance you'll get in QuickBooks is through the Help window, so let's first take a look at using it.

1. Choose Help > Help Index. You'll see the Help system index on the screen as shown in Figure 1.10.

Figure 1.10 The Help system index.

2. Type the first word or two of the topic you're looking for and the list of topics below scrolls automatically.

3. Double-click the name of the topic you want to read about and you'll see the Help window shown in Figure 1.11.

Figure 1.11 The Help window showing help text about the Create Invoices form.

The window contents will change depending on what sort of help information you're viewing, but the buttons at the top of the Help window stay the same:

*   **Index** displays a list of specific Help entries in alphabetical order, as shown in Figure 1.10. You can search for an entry by typing a word or two in this window. The list will automatically scroll to the topic name that most closely matches what you typed. To display a topic, just double-click it.

*   **Back** returns you to the Help topic you viewed previously.

*   **Options** is a menu button that lets you print, annotate, or otherwise work with Help information. See "Help Window Options" below.

To learn more about using the Help window:

1. Click the Index button at the top of the window to display the main topic list, as in Figure 1.10.

2. Type **help**. The index list will scroll to a selection of help topics.

3. Double-click the How to Use topic under Help.

Managing the Help Window

The Help system is a separate program from QuickBooks. You can open, close, minimize, maximize, and scroll the Help window just as you would a window in any other program. You can also move and resize the window in order to view instructions while putting them to use in QuickBooks.

Help Window Options

Pressing the Options menu button at the top of the Help window offers several commands for working with help information in other ways.

- **The Annotate command** lets you add a comment to a Help topic, perhaps a note to yourself or others that explains a procedure for your specific environment. When you add a comment, it appears as a paper clip icon next to the Help text you annotate. Just click the paper clip to open the annotation.

- **The Copy command** copies the current Help topic. This is a nice feature if you want to explain QuickBooks to someone else (your bookkeeper, perhaps) and you want to assemble a custom manual that contains only the topics that person needs to know. Just copy each topic and paste it into a word processor document and you'll soon have a booklet of printed instructions.

- **The Print Topic** command prints the current Help window contents on your printer.

- **The Font** command lets you change the size of type used in the Help window.

- **The Keep Help on Top** command gives you a choice about whether the Help window always stays on top of other windows on your screen.

- **The Use System Colors** command tells QuickBooks to use the same colors for the Help window's title bar as for all other windows on your computer, as set up with the Display control panel in Windows.

Help System Overviews

When you choose Help > Help On This Window, the Help window opens and displays an overview of the screen window or form that is currently active on your screen as shown in Figure 1.11 (page 33).

You can also press F1, click the Help button in a dialog box, or click the Help icon in the QuickBooks Iconbar (if it's showing) to display the same overview information you would see with the Help On This Window command.

Tip: *Any term or phrase that is displayed with green text in the Help window has an explanation or definition attached to it. Click the term or phrase to display a definition or explanation.*

QuickBooks and Your Industry

QuickBooks comes with nearly two dozen documents you can view or print that help you set up the program for your type of business. When you choose Help > QuickBooks and Your Industry, you'll see a list of industry documents. You can then select and view the document about your particular industry.

Each industry-specific document is about 25 pages long. It contains lots of specific suggestions for billing, recording expenses, tracking job costs, setting up your payroll, managing inventory, and handling other aspects of your business with QuickBooks. Read through this document and make notes about the parts that apply to your business. You may want to display certain topics in your industry document and print them to have on hand while you are going through the setup interview.

QuickBooks Professional Advisors

Many accountants and bookkeepers are registered with Intuit as Quick-Books advisors. To locate a list of advisors in your area, choose Help > Locate Advisors in Your Area. You'll be connected to the QuickBooks Small Business Online Web site where you can search for local advisors by state, city, and ZIP code. (See "Using Online Features in QuickBooks" below for more information.)

QuickBooks Small Business Online

By choosing Help > QuickBooks Small Business Online, you'll be taken to a Web site that's a fantastic information resource for your business. It offers a collection of articles by professionals about accounting, management, and other topics, as well as links to the QuickBooks tax table update, payroll, and online banking services, plus links to other sites that sell office supplies, furniture, computers and software, and other business essentials. (See "Using Online Features in QuickBooks" for more information.)

Hiding and Showing QCards

As you work with QuickBooks, you'll notice QCards, little yellow windows on the screen that contain brief explanations of the features you're using. These can be helpful at first, but after a while they get in your way. You can drag any QCard window around by its top edge or put it away by clicking the close box at its upper-right corner. To hide all QCards in the program:

1. Choose Edit > Preferences to display the Preferences dialog box.

2. Click the General icon in the scrolling list at the left side of the dialog box to display this group of options.

3. Check the Hide QCards In All Windows checkbox at the bottom.

About QuickBooks

Choosing Help > About QuickBooks simply displays the program's version number and some information about its development.

About Tax Table

Choosing Help > About Tax Table tells you which version of the tax table is currently installed. It also lets you go online to find out more about the QuickBooks tax table subscription service or to subscribe to the service.

Using Online Features in QuickBooks

Some components of the QuickBooks Help system and the features on the Online menu are located on the World Wide Web (Web). You'll need to connect your computer to a modem and a telephone line before using these services. You also need an Internet access account with an Internet Service Provider (ISP) and a Web browser program installed on your computer.

Setting Up an Online Account

The first time you choose a menu command that requires the use of online information or services, you'll start the Internet Connection Setup wizard. (You can also use the wizard at any time by choosing Online > Internet Connection Setup.)

If you have an online account, you can enter the information about it as the wizard asks you for it. If you don't have an online account, Intuit has arranged for you to get an account for free, but you can use it only to access Intuit's Web sites. If you choose the free account, you'll be given an option to open a paying account with the same ISP that will give you unfettered access to the Internet.

Installing a Web Browser

The Internet Connection Setup wizard also checks your computer to see if you have a Web browser installed on your computer. You must have at least version 3 of Netscape Navigator or Microsoft Internet Explorer in order to use all the features of the Intuit Web sites. If you have more than one browser installed on your computer, you can choose which one to use during Intuit Web connections. If you don't have the latest version of Microsoft Internet Explorer, you'll be given the chance to upgrade and the wizard will install it for you from the QuickBooks CD. Don't worry—the wizard automatically transfers all your custom settings (favorite places and so on) from your older version of Internet Explorer to the new one.

Intuit's Web Resources

Depending on the command you choose in QuickBooks, you can access a number of different resources.

- **Free 24-hour QuickBooks help**. Use Intuit's online technical support database to get answers to frequently asked questions (FAQs), product information updates, and other information.

- **Professional Advisor directory**. Search for professional QuickBooks advisors in your area.

- **Small business information**. Browse a repository of articles about small business management, or choose links to other sites that offer small business products and services.

- **Quicken Business CashFinder**. Find out the best rates for business loans and lines of credit.

- **Tax table updates**. Subscribe to Intuit's tax table update service.

- **QuickBooks updates**. Download interim releases of QuickBooks that offer better performance or bug fixes.

In addition, Intuit is offering a full payroll service to a limited number of QuickBooks owners during 1998. You can simply transmit your payroll information to an online site, and the service prepares your payroll checks with guaranteed accuracy.

If you don't have an Internet setup, we encourage you to get connected so you can take advantage of Intuit's vast collection of small business resources and services.

BOOKKEEPING BASICS

Accounting is keeping track of all the monetary details of your business. All the money you have, spend, receive, or owe can be divided into two main groups with a total of six categories:

Money you have or are owed, which can be subdivided as

- **Income**—money you take in during normal business operations.

- **Current assets**—cash on hand.

- **Fixed assets**—equipment, buildings, or land.

- **Equity**—amount of money you would net if you sold the business.

Money you spend or owe, which can be subdivided as

- **Expenses**—monthly costs such as payroll, utilities, and insurance.

- **Liabilities**—long-term debts such as mortgages and loans.

If accounting were just a matter of assigning all of your transactions to one of these six categories, of course, your ten-year-old could handle it for you. But it's not that simple, which is why most people use computers to take care of it. Within each of these six categories are dozens of subcategories that specifically describe each of your transactions. An accounting program makes it much easier to set up all those subcategories and ensure that every one of your financial details gets assigned to the right one.

Every time you pay an employee, close a sale, or make a bank deposit or a loan payment, that's a detail that has to be recorded. For example, you have to track telephone expenses as such within the expenses category or else you'll have no idea how much you're spending on phone bills. You also have to track sales taxes as such within the liabilities category or else you won't know how much to send the state government each month or each quarter.

It's as if each category is a file drawer and each subcategory is a folder inside one of those drawers. As you conduct business each day, each of your activities can be classified as a type of transaction in its own subcategory, or folder, in one of your six file drawers. For example:

- Whenever you write a check, spend money, lick a stamp, or make a phone call, a record for each of these expenses needs to be put into the proper folder inside your Expenses drawer.

- Each time you sell a widget or install a bathtub, you receive money for this, and a record needs to be put in the proper folder in your Income drawer.

- If you borrow money through a mortgage or a small business loan, or if you collect sales tax from customers, you must file a record in the right folder in your Liabilities drawer.

- If you borrow cash or buy property, the market value of the property or cash is added to a folder in your Assets drawers.

- As you make payments to your mortgage company, you reduce the amount owed in the mortgage record in the Liabilities drawer, and you increase the value of the building in the Fixed Assets folder in the Assets drawer.

All this sorting and tracking is a pain, which is why there's such a robust market for computerized accounting programs. They help you with all aspects of your accounting in several ways:

- They organize every transaction in the proper folder in the proper drawer. In an accounting system, these categories are called a chart of accounts.

- They capture information by allowing you to handle the transactions or activities related to your accounting, such as writing checks, making deposits, decreasing a liability, or increasing the value of an asset.

- They make the information you collect and categorize readily available in reports for your tax collector, your investors, your accountant, or yourself.

Most accounting programs are organized by these three basic aspects of accounting: a chart of accounts, activities, and reports. QuickBooks is no different, but before we get into how QuickBooks handles these basic accounting chores, let's look at them in more detail.

The Chart of Accounts

The *chart of accounts* (see Figure 2.1) is the system of categories and subcategories you use to organize all of your transactions properly.

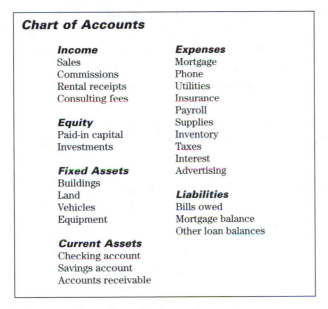

Chart of Accounts

Income	**Expenses**
Sales	Mortgage
Commissions	Phone
Rental receipts	Utilities
Consulting fees	Insurance
	Payroll
Equity	Supplies
Paid-in capital	Inventory
Investments	Taxes
	Interest
Fixed Assets	Advertising
Buildings	
Land	**Liabilities**
Vehicles	Bills owed
Equipment	Mortgage balance
	Other loan balances
Current Assets	
Checking account	
Savings account	
Accounts receivable	

Figure 2.1 An outline of a chart of accounts.

Notice how the chart of accounts is set up in the six main categories with subcategories under each of them. *Income categories* are for recording and organizing monies you receive on a day-to-day basis. Subcategories for different types of income include sales, commissions, rental receipts, and consulting fees.

Equity categories are where you track the value of your vested interest in your company. If you sold the company tomorrow and cashed out all its assets, the equity is the money that would be left over after all debts were paid. In equity categories, you keep track of the money you invest in the company (paid in capital) and the money you take out as an investor (owner's draws). If you make a profit, it goes into an equity category called "retained earnings," and if you lose money, the retained earnings category is debited.

Fixed assets categories are items such as buildings, land, and equipment. In these categories (as opposed to the equity categories), you track the current market value of each asset, rather than just your equity in them.

Current assets are rapidly changing asset accounts, such as a checking account, a savings account, or your accounts receivables.

Expenses are day-to-day costs such as phone bills, fuel, payroll, office supplies, and mortgage payments.

Liabilities are debts, including the balances of mortgages, business loans, taxes due, bills received but not yet paid, or other debts owed.

The chart of accounts is the nerve center of your accounting system. It's the one place where every financial transaction is recorded in some way. In QuickBooks, the chart of accounts handles tedious accounting chores automatically so you don't have to think about them. For example, when you make a mortgage payment, you simply fill out a check form with the proper amount. After you fill out the check form, though, QuickBooks will do the following:

- Print a check for it that automatically includes your loan account number, the lender's name and address, and even the correct amount if it's the same every month

- Record the payment in the proper expense categories (principal and interest would be separate categories, as would taxes and insurance if these are included as part of your mortgage payment)

- Deduct the amount of the payment from your checking account in the current assets category.

- Reduce the liability account for that mortgage by the amount of principal in the payment

- Increase the equity account for the building on which the mortgage is held by the amount of principal in the payment.

In this way, you always know exactly how much you owe on the building, how much your equity in the building is, and how much interest and principal you've paid in the current year.

QuickBooks suggests a chart of accounts based on the type of business you tell it you have, but you can add, change, or delete categories and sub-categories to tailor it further. Once you've set up your chart of accounts, you're ready to begin tracking your business activities.

Activities

Activities are the things you do every day, week, or month. Every time you receive money, spend money, order inventory, create invoices, or pay employees, you record this activity in a QuickBooks form, and it pigeon-holes the activity in the proper category and subcategory in your chart of accounts. A quick look at the Activities menu in QuickBooks (or the flow-chart icons in the QuickBooks Navigator) gives you an idea of the different activities you can perform.

Reports

Reports are snapshots of your business activity for a certain period of time. For example, a payroll report might show what you paid each employee dur-ing a quarter, or a tax report might show what you owe in quarterly sales taxes. You use reports to understand the health of your business, to compile information for paying taxes, and to apply for financing. A sample profit and loss (P&L) statement is shown in Figure 2.2.

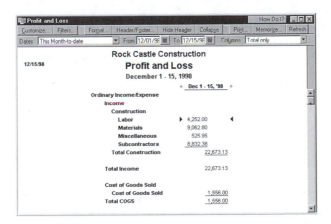

Figure 2.2
A sample profit and loss statement.

This report shows a company's current profit or loss as of a certain date. These statements are usually required for bank loans.

By setting up a chart of accounts that contains enough categories to organize your financial transactions properly, and by recording those transactions faithfully, you can collect all the data necessary to produce accurate, up-to-date reports on your business at any time.

How QuickBooks Handles Accounting

QuickBooks is organized by lists, activities, and reports. There's a menu for each of these key components at the top of your screen, so the program's operations are neatly categorized for you. Let's take a look.

The Lists Menu

Lists are places where you store information that you use regularly in QuickBooks, such as your expense and income categories and other important business data. All lists are available from the Lists menu, which is shown in Figure 2.3.

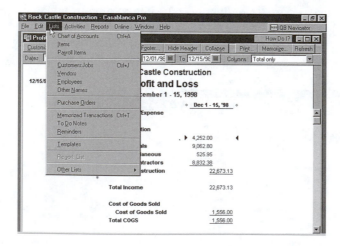

Figure 2.3
The Lists menu.

The chart of accounts is one type of list. Other lists store information about employees, inventory items, customers, vendors, and more. The lists you'll use frequently are discussed below.

Chart of Accounts

The Chart of Accounts list is where you keep track of all your income, expense, asset, and liability categories. You can have up to 10,000 categories in your chart of accounts. See Figure 1.6 (page 26) for an example.

Items

The Items list is where you describe the goods or services you buy and sell. This includes inventory, services, sales tax, labor charges, discounts, and other categories you can set up to track the types of goods or services for which you collect money. For example, an art gallery might list oil paintings, photographs, and sculptures along with framing, shipping, and sales tax. An advertising agency might have different types of services for which it charges clients different rates. The Items list can contain up to 16,000 items (including inventory items). Figure 2.4 shows a typical list of construction labor items.

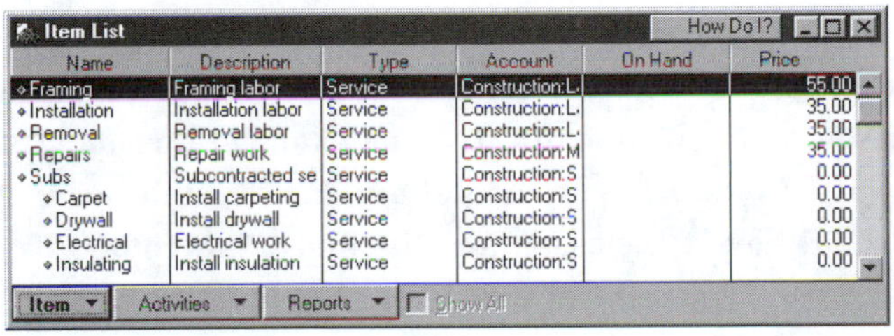

Figure 2.4 An Item list from a sample file.

In the Type column, you can have several kinds of items. Service items are different categories of charges for labor, such as framing labor and installation labor. Inventory part items are goods you sell, such as doorknobs. Non-inventory parts are goods you use on jobs but don't track in inventory (such as lumber) or goods you specifically purchase for a customer.

Payroll Items

The Payroll Item list contains items related to paychecks, such as salary, withholding, deductions, and company contributions, so you can track how much you spend in each category. Figure 2.5 shows an example of a Payroll Item list.

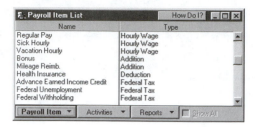

Figure 2.5 A sample Payroll Item list.

Customer:Job

The Customer:Job list (see Figure 2.6) includes the names, addresses, and other contact information for all of your customers.

USING CLASSES

When you want to track income or expenses other than by employee, vendor, customer, or job, you can use classes. Classes let you assign expenses and income to broader categories. If you're in the construction business, for example, you might set up classes for Remodeling Jobs and for New Construction so you could track income by each type of work. You can even set up subclasses under each class. If you have an art gallery, for example, your Paintings class could have subclasses for Oils and Watercolors. If you have several stores, you can track sales in each store by class.

QuickBooks gives you the option to use classes when you're completing the setup interview (see Chapter 4, "Setting Up Your Business."). If you decide to use classes, the forms you use to write checks, create invoices, enter bills, and perform other activities will include options to specify a class or subclass for each transaction.

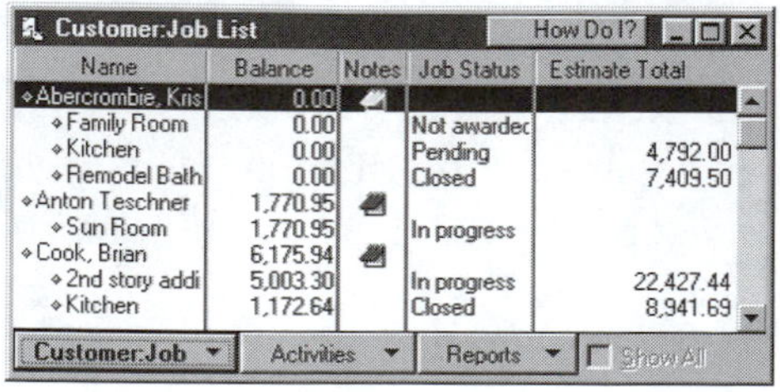

Figure 2.6 A sample Customer:Job list.

The list is called Customer:Job because you can specify several individual jobs for one customer. For example, if you're a builder and you specialize in framing houses, you might have a big customer that is building several houses in one subdivision. With the Customer:Job list, you can identify each house you're framing as an individual job to track its profit or loss. If your business is printing, one of your customers might be a hospital that provides you with many different jobs, such as printing menus, nursing schedules, parking lot assignments, or chart forms.

Vendors

Vendors provide services, materials, and the things you sell. When you add a vendor's name to the Vendors list, QuickBooks allows you to add addresses, contact names, phone numbers, and discount information at the same time. You can also specify whether this vendor is eligible to receive a 1099 form at year's end. After that, this information prints automatically on purchase orders and checks when you specify the vendor's name. The Vendor List window (see Figure 2.7) shows only vendor names and the outstanding balance you owe each one.

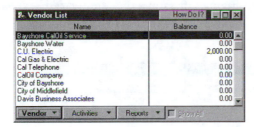

Figure 2.7 The Vendor List window.

Employees

The Employees list keeps track of all of the relevant information about your employees. This includes each person's name, salary or hourly wage rate, hire date, social security number, address, marital status, and number of dependents or exemptions for tax reporting. There's also a section that can be customized to include an email address, spouse's name, birthday, and so on; you can even keep notes about the employee's performance. Figure 2.8 shows a form where you would enter employee information.

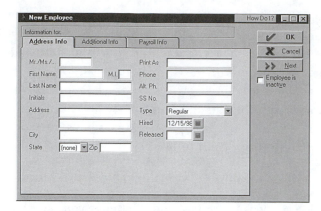

Figure 2.8 A New Employee form.

Notice you can also check a box at the right to list the employee as inactive. When you do this, the employee no longer shows up on the standard Employees list unless you choose Show All Employees with the Employee menu button.

Memorized Transactions

Memorized Transactions is a list of transactions that recur (for example, monthly loan payments). Figure 2.9 shows the Memorized Transaction List window.

Figure 2.9
The Memorized Transaction List window.

Once you tell QuickBooks to memorize a transaction, you can enter that transaction by simply selecting it from the list and choosing the Enter Transaction command with the Memorized Transaction menu button at the bottom of the list window. This is very helpful with complex transactions such as mortgage payments, in which the total amount is split among several accounts such as interest, escrow, and principal payments.

Reminders

The Reminders list reminds you when to perform certain accounting activities. Figure 2.10 displays a typical list.

Figure 2.10 A sample Reminders list.

This list is automatically generated, based on what bills, checks, invoices, or other activities you have outstanding or due. If you have pending reminders, this list appears automatically whenever you open your company data file.

> **Tip:** *If you don't want the Reminders list to show up each time you open your company file, choose File > Preferences, click the Reminders icon at the left, and uncheck the Show Reminders List checkbox.*

As you work, you will refer to lists constantly to enter your transactions, as you'll see below and in Chapter 6, "Daily Activities."

The Activities Menu

The Activities menu (see Figure 2.11) is where you handle day-to-day accounting tasks such as writing checks, making deposits, creating invoices, and making purchase orders.

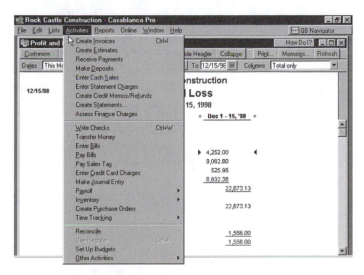

Figure 2.11
The Activities menu.

Each type of activity brings up a window containing a form. You simply fill in the form and QuickBooks automatically debits and credits the appropriate categories in your chart of accounts. To record a bill you've received from a vendor, for example, you would select Activities > Enter Bills. You would then enter the vendor's information, such as a reference number, date due, and terms for discount (if any). The bill will then appear in your Reminders list, in that vendor's records as an outstanding debt, and on your chart of accounts in the appropriate accounts payable category.

Writing checks is another common activity. For example, suppose you want to write a check to your mortgage company. You would use the Write Checks form, which is shown in Figure 2.12.

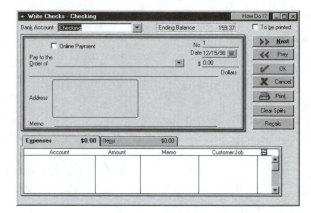

Figure 2.12 The Write Checks form.

The top part of this form is the check. The date line automatically contains today's date; you can change it if you like. Once you type the first few characters of your mortgage company's name, the rest of it is automatically filled in, because you've recorded this company name in your Vendors list (see "Vendors," page 47). You then fill out the numeric amount of the payment; the written-out amount is filled out automatically.

In the lower part of the window, you assign the payment to one or more expense categories. Since this payment is for a mortgage, the total payment would be broken up into several different categories (principal, interest, and property taxes).

Note: *After you've assigned expense categories to a vendor one time, QuickBooks remembers the categories so you don't have to fill them out again the next time you write a check to the same vendor (although with mortgage interest and principal, you'll change the amounts every month).*

When you click the OK or Next button, you're done. The check register will show the recorded transaction. If you look into your Interest Expense account's register, you'll see that the amount of interest from this payment has been added. If you want a report of all your interest expenses, QuickBooks will provide it. As you'll see in Chapter 8, "Using Reports and Graphs," you can use a report filter to select interest expenses only and produce a list of check numbers, dates, and payees.

Tip: *To see a list of interest expenses without producing a report, choose Edit > Find and then select the Interest Expense account as the filter. For more information, see "Finding transactions" in Chapter 6.*

The Reports Menu

The Reports menu is where you turn when you need current, detailed information about your business. You also use the Graphs submenu to create one of six different types of graphs that present your financial data visually. Figure 2.13 displays the Reports menu.

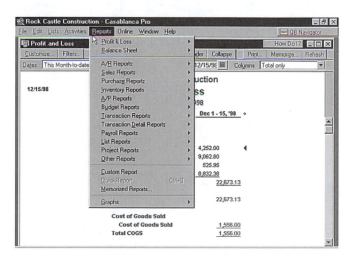

Figure 2.13 The Reports menu.

There are many different reports contained within each category on this menu, and they can all be customized. For example, you might want to print a sales report for the whole year, for a certain quarter, for a month, or even for a few days. You can also customize such a sales report to contain information concerning only one item, or only one salesperson. Figure 2.14 displays a sales report listed by customer.

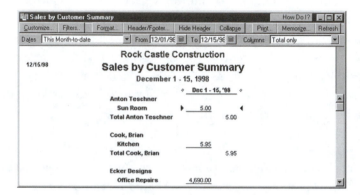

Figure 2.14
A sales report by customer.

QuickBooks offers more than 100 different reports, each of which can be customized to show you or someone else exactly the information you need to manage or evaluate your business. We'll explore reports and graphs in detail in Chapter 8, "Using Reports and Graphs."

PLANNING YOUR QUICKBOOKS CONVERSION

Setting up a computerized accounting system can be a frightening experience, even if other aspects of your business are already computerized. When you start, you're not sure how much time it will involve or what kinds of changes it will mean for your day-to-day operations. In this chapter, we'll help you develop a step-by-step strategy for making the transition to QuickBooks. You'll learn which records you'll need on hand as you set up QuickBooks, and then we'll give you an overview of how the setup process works and suggest a schedule to follow so you know what's in store and can plan the time to make it work.

After reading this chapter, you'll be ready to go through the actual setup process in Chapter 4, "Setting Up Your Business."

To make the transition to QuickBooks, you need three key ingredients:

1. A computer system and the QuickBooks software.

2. Enough time to set up the program and enter your data.

3. The business records where you currently store customer, vendor, employee, asset, equity, liability, income, and expense information.

Your Computer System

QuickBooks will run on just about any Windows-compatible PC made since 1993. Here are the minimum hardware requirements.

*   486-based PC-compatible computer or better.

- Microsoft Windows 95 or Microsoft Windows NT 4.0 or later.

- 32MB (megabytes) of RAM (random access memory).

- 45MB of free hard disk space (55MB for QuickBooks Pro, and add an extra 40MB if you choose to install Internet Explorer 4.0 with either version of QuickBooks).

- 256-color graphics.

- Any printer that's compatible with Windows 95 or Windows NT 4.0.

- A modem, if you want to get online information and updates from Intuit.

- A 2x (double-speed) CD-ROM drive or faster.

 Tip: *If you need further clarification of the computer hardware requirements, consult the Getting Started guide that comes in the QuickBooks software package.*

These are the minimum requirements. Your QuickBooks system will run faster on newer computers such as Pentium-based PCs, and on computers with more than 32MB of RAM.

 Note: *If you want QuickBooks to handle your payroll, you must have the latest version of the federal and state tax tables installed with your software. Your QuickBooks CD-ROM includes the latest tax tables as of the time it was produced, and you can subscribe to more updates by choosing Online > Tax Table Service to navigate to the QuickBooks Web site. A subscription for a year's worth of tax table updates costs $59.95.*

Networked Multiuser Setups

If you plan to have several people use QuickBooks on a network, you'll need to buy a separate copy of the program for each user. QuickBooks is optimized for multiuser operations on networks that run on Windows 95/NT peer to peer, Windows NT Server, or Novell Netware software. (See Appendix A, "Multiuser Features in QuickBooks Pro," for more information.)

Backup Strategies

Since your accounting system is the nerve center of your business, we also recommend that you have an adequate backup strategy in effect from the first day you begin using QuickBooks. This means making a daily backup copy of your QuickBooks data file. QuickBooks itself will occasionally remind you to back up your data file, but you should get in the habit of doing this every day.

You can start out by backing up your data on floppy disks, but it's faster and easier to use a higher-density medium such as a Zip, Jaz, or Syquest drive, which holds anywhere from 100MB to a gigabyte or more on a single disk.

It's also a good idea to keep your backup copies in a separate location, such as your home or a safe deposit box. After all, you can always replace your computer if it's stolen or burned in a fire, but you can't replace your data without spending all the time you invested to store it in the first place.

We know of some companies that maintain two backups: one at the office and one at home. Each night they make a backup at the office and then take that copy home, bringing back the home copy the following day. If you follow this strategy, you always have one backup that's current and one that's only a day old, and you'll have the copies in two different locations. In the worst case—your hard disk crashes and your newest backup disk becomes corrupted—you'll still only lose one day's worth of data.

SECURING YOUR DATA

Your accounting system isn't necessarily everyone's business. QuickBooks lets you set up several levels of passwords to control access to different sets of information. For example, you can set an overall administrator password that provides access to all your data as well as other passwords that allow different access levels or data-handling privileges for different users. For more information, see "Creating User Names and Passwords" in Chapter 5.

Finding the Time to Set Up

QuickBooks will make it much easier for you to gather vital financial information every day and to see how your business is doing at any particular time, but it doesn't work automatically. If technology were advanced to the point where we'd like it to be, you would be able to pile your paper records on top of the QuickBooks package at night and return in the morning with your system all set up and ready to go. Sadly, though, computers aren't that capable just yet. Somebody has to install the program and input your financial data, and that person is probably you.

The number-one reason business owners never manage to get going with QuickBooks is that they don't feel they have enough time. We know that you're busy, but if you ever hope to realize any benefits from computerized accounting, you must make the commitment to go through with the whole setup process, and then to record your daily financial activities faithfully with QuickBooks. Setting up and maintaining your accounting system is just as important as anything else you do during a day.

Fortunately, you can be completely set up in a few days and those days don't have to be consecutive. All you have to do is make the commitment to set aside five days. If you're already well organized, you can do it in less time. As you read this chapter, you'll get a better idea of the time commitment you'll need to make for your own situation and you'll be able to determine just when you can spend that time.

MAKING QUICKBOOKS YOUR PRINTER

Printing checks is a handy feature of QuickBooks, but you don't have to use it if you prefer to write checks by hand. We recommend the check-printing feature if you write more than 25 checks a month; it saves time and it gives your checks a professional appearance. QuickBooks also allows you to print invoices, purchase orders, or labels on preprinted forms, your company letterhead, or plain paper.

You can order paper supplies such as blank checks or invoice forms through Intuit (ordering information is in the box), or you can use other suppliers such as Office Max, Office Depot, or mail-order firms like Viking Office Products or Current. If you're going to use the check-printing feature, order your checks a couple of weeks before you intend to start using QuickBooks so they'll be available immediately when you need them. We also recommend using window envelopes for sending checks or invoices to those pesky vendors who don't provide return envelopes—QuickBooks forms are set up so the vendor's address will appear in the right place on checks and invoices.

As for the other forms, we recommend printing them on plain paper at the beginning until you get them formatted exactly the way you want. When you print forms on plain paper, QuickBooks will fill in your company name and address in the header if you like. You can always order preprinted invoices and other forms later.

Setting Your Start Date

Your first order of business in planning a move to QuickBooks is to set a start date. This is the date when you begin recording your daily business activities with QuickBooks. You then collect paper records back to that date and enter them into QuickBooks to bring your system up to the present day. For example, if you're reading this in October, you may set September 1 as your start date. If so, you'll need to collect sales, expense, and other activity records from today back to September 1 and enter them all into QuickBooks to bring the system up to date.

With a start date in mind, you can then plan the process of collecting your records, installing QuickBooks, setting up the program, and entering historical data.

Give your start date some thought because your setup will depend on knowing this date. Many people use the beginning of their company's fiscal year or of a calendar year, but your start date can be any date for which you will have complete records from that point on. If you prepare balance sheets regularly, you may find it handy to use the date of your most recent one as your start date.

 Tip: Once you settle on a start date, stick to it. It's much easier to determine your start date at the beginning than to change it after setting up QuickBooks.

USE YOUR ACCOUNTANT

Your accountant can be a big help as you make the transition to QuickBooks. Before you start planning your transition (and as you go through it), ask your accountant for advice. You can get help with choosing a start date, setting up income and expense accounts, and locating historical data that you'll need to enter when you set up QuickBooks.

You may also find that with QuickBooks you'll be able to perform some tasks yourself that you previously paid a bookkeeper or service to do, such as preparing your weekly payroll or preparing 1099 forms at the end of the year.

The Five-Day Setup Schedule

The time required for setting up QuickBooks will vary, of course, depending on how many vendors, customers, and inventory items you have. But you should be able to handle the whole process in five days. A suggested schedule is outlined next.

Day 1: The Interview

QuickBooks allows you to set up your company all at once through the EasyStep Interview, or you can set up various accounts and lists as you go. We strongly recommend the interview process because it automatically creates accounts and items that are specific to your business, and it provides a good overview of the kinds of information you'll need to deal with. You should be able to complete the interview in two or three hours. We'll tackle it in Chapter 4, "Setting Up Your Business."

WHEN TO SCHEDULE DAY 1

Completing the interview requires a lot of concentration, so don't plan to do it during a normal business day. Rather, plan it for a day or evening when you won't be disturbed by customers or employees. Other days in the setup process can be worked into your normal schedule, but not Day 1.

Day 2: Fine-Tuning Accounts and Entering Historical Transactions

On this day, you'll fine-tune the chart of accounts that was initially set up as a result of your responses to interview questions in Day 1, and then you'll enter historical transactions that have taken place between your start date and the present day.

Fine-Tuning Your Accounts

This is the time to review the chart of accounts carefully and make any changes you want so the accounts perfectly reflect your company's financial activity. Set aside about two hours when you can concentrate and won't be interrupted.

In many cases, you'll use this time to set up more subcategories in your chart of accounts so you can more accurately track income and expenses. In the sample construction company file shown in Figure 3.1, there are several subaccounts under the Construction income accounts.

Figure 3.1 A chart of accounts for a construction company with subaccounts shown. The company owner can use subaccounts to track income by specific types of services.

It's vital for you to create the account categories you'll need before you begin entering transactions. If you don't, you'll have to go back and redo mislabeled transactions one by one, and you won't be able to delete any improper accounts until you've reassigned any transactions that were originally assigned to them.

Tip: *See our suggestions in Appendix B, "Customizing QuickBooks for Your Business," for help with this setup for a company like yours. Also, it's a good idea to print the whole chart of accounts and have your accountant review it before you begin entering transactions.*

Adding Historical Transactions

After the fine-tuning process, you'll be ready to enter the purchase and sales transactions that have occurred between your start date and today. If your existing records are well organized, you can manage this activity in piecemeal fashion—entering a transaction or two at a time, getting on with other business duties, and then going back to the computer.

Day 3: Payroll and Bank Accounts

Setting up your basic payroll information is easy in QuickBooks; for a small company, it shouldn't take very long. The EasyStep Interview will allow you to set up a master employee template so that all your standard payroll information is entered once. After that, you'll only have to enter the data that changes for each employee as necessary.

But along with standard information, you'll also have to enter paycheck data for all your employees from the beginning of the year. You'll need a payroll report for this so you can enter the year-to-date wages and other payroll items for all of your employees. We suggest you enter the basic payroll information for each employee on Day 3, leaving the process of entering historical data for another day. Finally, you'll also use this day to finish entering bank account information that wasn't automatically taken care of when you entered your historical transactions on Day 2.

By the time you're finished with Day 3, your QuickBooks system should contain most of the historical financial data from your start date to the present day. The next two days will be spent in completing the unfinished customer, inventory, and payroll records that you began earlier.

Day 4: Completing Customer and Vendor Data

During the EasyStep Interview, you entered data on only a few customers and vendors because you wanted to get on with the rest of the process. Now is the time to enter the rest of your customer and vendor data. You don't have to enter all of the data at one sitting, but this is a good time to get the bulk of it done so you won't have to take the extra time during a transaction later on. You may want to get a data-entry clerk to do this task if you have many customers or vendors.

This data entry can be a lengthy and tedious process, but once the customers and vendors are entered you have instant recall of their information for invoices, sales slips, and address labels. As you acquire new customers or choose new vendors, you can add their information at any time.

 Tip: If you want to track sales by employee or associate customers with specific employee sales reps, set up your payroll information before entering all the customer data—you'll need the employee names on hand before you can assign customers to specific sales reps.

Day 5: Completing the Item List

As you go through the interview process, QuickBooks prompts you to enter the items for which you receive money, such as sales from inventory, labor, non-inventory parts, shipping, and various types of services. Today you'll return to your list of items and finish filling it out. If you plan to track inventory with QuickBooks, you'll also add your inventory items and the number of each on hand.

First, complete the list of items you sell. You can store up to 14,500 items in QuickBooks. If your list is extensive, you might want to assign this task to a data-entry clerk. You will need to have this list fairly complete before you begin ordering items or selling them. Remember to add items for subtotals, markups, and discounts if you need them.

> ***Tip:*** *An item called Subtotal is important if you want to show subtotals of materials or labor on invoices, for example. See Chapter 7, "Weekly and Monthly Activities," for more information on using subtotals.*

After going through this setup schedule, you'll be ready to begin using QuickBooks for your day-to-day business. You'll find that using purchase orders, invoices, sales forms, and paying bills or writing checks will be much simpler than before.

Gathering Your Records

Whether your business records are all neatly filed in a group of folders or scattered in several locations at more than one office, you'll invest a fair amount of time just collecting them for QuickBooks. The rest of this chapter tells you what kinds of records you need, but let's talk first about how to gather and organize them.

To collect your records most efficiently, go through the lists of documents below and choose the kinds of documents that you can most easily lay your hands on first. Take one record category at a time—for example, collect all of your bank statements before moving on to your tax ID numbers.

As you go along, you'll probably find that you're accomplishing more than one task at a time. For example, that old tax return showing your tax ID number will also contain schedules that help you determine expense categories for your chart of accounts. But try to stay focused on the information category you're currently working on rather than getting sidetracked by other types of information.

As you locate the records in each category, put them into separate labeled folders or envelopes, then store them near the computer you'll be using to set up QuickBooks.

Here are some folders you might set up and the types of information they'll contain. You can use them as a checklist as you gather your records.

General Business Data

- Federal and state Employer ID numbers.

- Fiscal year-end date.

- QuickBooks start date (See "Setting Your Start Date" in this chapter and "Choosing Conversion and Start Dates" in Chapter 4).

- Chart of accounts categories or your current chart of accounts, if you have one.

- A budget for the company fiscal year, if any.

- Total income and expenses from your start date or for the current fiscal year.

Assets

- A list of invoices outstanding as of the QuickBooks start date.

- The total amount each customer owes you as of your start date.

- Amounts of bank balances as of your start date. For this information you will need to collect the most recent statements from all bank accounts, including checking, savings, certificates of deposit, and money market funds. Be sure to have a record of all uncleared checks, deposits, or other items as of your start date as well. These statements should agree with your check registers or at least match them as closely as possible.

- The current value of all your assets, including inventory, as of your start date. If you have a balance sheet from your accountant, start with that; otherwise, make your best guess. You can always change this figure later.

- Your equity in the company, which includes all the money you have put into the company, plus the sum of the retained earnings (the net profit or loss) for each year your company has been operating.

Any earnings (or loss) from before your start date will be assigned to the retained earnings account. (See Chapter 4.)

 Tip: *Use the ending balance on the last bank statement before your start date or you can use your latest balance sheet date as your start date and then take data off that balance sheet.*

Liabilities

*   A list of vendor invoices that have not been paid as of your Quick-Books start date.

*   The total amount you owe each vendor as of your start date.

*   Credit card statements. If you want to track charges to your credit cards, gather the last statements before your start date, plus any transactions prior to your start date that haven't shown up on any statements yet. (Remember that some charges may not show up for a couple of months.)

Vendors

*   A list of vendors, including addresses, contact names, and phone numbers, plus tax ID numbers for vendors who are eligible for 1099s.

Customers

*   Names, addresses, phone numbers and other information about current, regular customers (don't bother gathering data on one-time or long-ago customers).

Employees

*   Payroll information, including the following:

    *   A list of employees, including social security numbers, addresses, rates of pay, withholding allowances, and other regular additions or deductions from pay.

- Each employee's payroll totals for gross salary, taxes, other deductions or additions for the current calendar year, up to your start date.

- Each employee's accrued hours for sick and vacation time as of your start date.

- Types of regular additions to or deductions from employee pay (such as automobile reimbursements and insurance copayments).

- Your state's unemployment tax rate.

- Your status for credit toward federal unemployment tax (FUTA) and your state's disability insurance (SDI) rate.

Inventory

- A list of types of items you sell (products or services), the items themselves, their sale prices (or hourly rates), the quantities on hand, and whether the items are taxable.

Tip: If you maintain a large inventory, you may want to make your start date as of the last physical inventory you did so that you can enter proper quantities on hand.

Taxes

- Sales tax information if applicable—for example, city or county taxes collected, including the tax rates, tax codes, and agency names and addresses.

- The total amounts of sales taxes you owe as of your start date, and the names and addresses of agencies to which they are owed.

- The total amounts of payroll taxes you owe as of your start date, and the names and addresses of the agencies to which they are owed.

Standardizing List Names and Codes

Before beginning to enter data into QuickBooks for your company, there are some conventions you'll want to observe so that your data will be consistent and easy to use.

For vendors, use the company name ("Wildwood Appliances," for example) or use the last name first if the company name is a person's name ("Smith, Mary, CPA," for example). When you fill in the address area in the QuickBooks form, always use this format:

    Wildwood Appliances
    45 Wildwood Lane
    WINSLOW AZ 80000
    Attn: Mary Wildwood

Figure 3.2 shows how information on this vendor might look in the form for entering vendor information in QuickBooks.

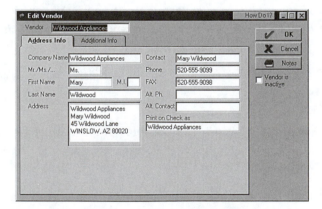

Figure 3.2 A vendor information form for Wildwood Appliances.

Note the capitalization of the city and state code. This format is consistent with that used by the US Postal Service and will be standardized for your 1099 forms, mailing labels, and window envelopes if you use them.

For individual customers or employees, use the last name first. (You can reverse the order when you print checks or invoices.) Use the company name for business customers.

ELIMINATING DUPLICATE NAMES

If for some reason you end up creating two versions of a customer, vendor, or employee name, you can really muck up your accounting system by entering transactions under different versions of the name at different times. If you find that you've done this, you can merge the data by following these steps:

1. *Choose the Vendors, Customers, or Employees list from the Lists menu.*

2. *Double-click the name that's duplicated to display the Edit Name form.*

3. *Edit the name so it's exactly like its duplicate and click the OK button. QuickBooks will ask you if you want to combine the transactions under the one name.*

4. *Click the Yes button to merge the transactions under one name.*

For items, you may use item numbers and names. Be sure that these names and numbers are unique to each item and are easily identifiable! You probably already have item numbers or names that work well for your business. If not, assign item names and numbers to your inventory now, before you need to enter them during the QuickBooks setup process.

Preparing Inventory and Sales Data

If your business sells many different items, entering all of these into the computer will probably be the most time-consuming part of the setup process. Once there, however, the items are available at a click of a mouse button to add to purchase orders, invoices, or sales forms, and they'll accurately reflect your inventory status in reports.

Here's how to tackle this job. First, gather your paper lists of inventory items. Determine a consistent name/number system that is instantly recognizable to you and your employees as descriptive of each item. You will need to set up three different accounts for inventory items:

- A purchase (or COGS, for Cost of Goods Sold) account for when you buy the item.

- • An income account for when you sell the item.

- • An asset account (to identify it in your inventory) for each item.

When you fill in the item form shown in Figure 3.3 you'll find spaces for this information.

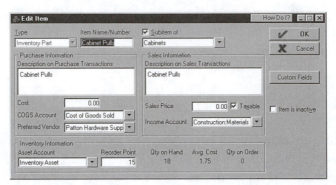

Figure 3.3 The Edit Item form used to enter information about inventory items.

Try to be as thorough as you can about laying your hands on all of the records listed in this chapter. It will make the setup process that much easier.

Okay—you're ready to set up your accounting system with QuickBooks. Set aside a few uninterrupted hours to complete the EasyStep Interview then take a deep breath and confront that computer. It's only a machine, after all, and it will help you take charge of your business as never before. Think of it as an accountant who knows your business intimately who you can also call up at any minute of the day or night and get the precise answers you need. In the next chapter, you'll turn your computer into an accountant with QuickBooks.

SETTING UP YOUR BUSINESS

In this chapter, you'll see how to set up QuickBooks for your business. But since setting up QuickBooks must begin at a specific time of the year, let's first consider when to make the switch from your current accounting system to QuickBooks.

Choosing Conversion and Start Dates

You can convert from paper to electronic bookkeeping at any time. Obviously, it's best to choose a time when you have some extra hours in which to go through the setup interview and enter your company's historical data.

How Much Data Do You Want to Have Available?

If you don't care about having a lot of historical data on hand for analysis in QuickBooks during your first year, make your start date as close to the present day as possible. The closer your start date is to the present day, the less historical data you'll need to enter.

On the other hand, if you want as much detail as possible about your business for the whole year, set your start date closer to (or on) January 1. You'll have to enter a lot of historical data, but that also means you'll have more of the current year's data from which to generate reports for analyzing the health of your business.

Note: *QuickBooks can easily import data from Quicken, QuickPay, or previous versions of QuickBooks. To import data from other accounting programs, you must convert the data into a format QuickBooks understands, usually by using a spreadsheet program. See "importing data" in the Help system index.*

But choosing when to convert also depends on other factors:

- When you can spare the time.

- What date you choose for your start date (the date you'll enter the first daily transactions into QuickBooks, which isn't usually the same as the conversion date).

- How much of a given year's historical business activity you'll want to enter.

Don't make the switch when you know you'll be busy doing other demanding projects such as preparing your taxes, figuring out quarterly reports, or taking inventory.

If you're well into the calendar year, you may want to convert to QuickBooks in midyear just to get the process rolling.

MAKING THE MOVE TO QUICKBOOKS

If you're upgrading to QuickBooks from Quicken, you'll be given the chance to import your Quicken data files into a new QuickBooks data file when you go through the setup interview. You can also import Quicken data into a new QuickBooks file at any other time by choosing an option in the program's startup dialog box. You can only use this process once for each file, however; don't plan to continue recording data in Quicken and then transfer it again later on. For more details about preparing your Quicken data for transfer to QuickBooks, see "Quicken" in the Help system index.

Completing the Interview

Now let's get into the details of setting up your company. The best way to do this is to complete the EasyStep Interview, which takes you through all the decisions you need to make about how your company is set up.

1. Select New Company from the File menu. You'll automatically be taken to the new company interview.

 Note: *If you really don't want to do the interview, you can bypass it by clicking the Skip Interview button on the third Interview screen. If you do this, you'll then be presented with a series of dialog boxes where you fill in information about your company. We don't recommend this method, though, because you won't get any of the helpful explanations that you'll need to make the right choices about setting up the program.*

2. The opening screen is a welcome message. Click the Next button. You'll then be asked if you are upgrading from Quicken or an earlier version of QuickBooks, by a screen that looks like the one shown in Figure 4.1.

Figure 4.1 The EasyStep Interview helps you set up your company by answering questions.

3. Click the appropriate radio button then click the Next button.

Note: *We won't take you screen by screen through the whole process, but we will show selected screens to give you an idea of what you'll be doing.*

How the Interview Is Organized

The interview is divided into seven main parts. Along the right side of the screen are tabs that show which main part you're currently working in. (We're in the General section of the interview in the example above.) You can click on a tab to jump to another part of the interview at any time.

Note: *Complete the General section before going on to other areas. QuickBooks won't know enough about your company to present the rest of the interview questions unless you fill in your basic company information and start date first.*

Along the top of the window, another set of tabs indicates which subsection of the part you're currently working on. You can click these tabs to jump to other subsections. As you complete each subsection or part, its tab will show a checkmark to indicate that the section is finished.

Tip: *Once you've filled in your company information, you can leave the interview at any time and return later. Just open your company data file and choose File > EasyStep Interview; QuickBooks will always remember the information you entered previously.*

At the beginning of each part and subsection, there's an introductory screen that explains what you'll do next. Following the introduction, you choose options or enter information about your company. On many screens, there's a More button that looks like the one shown in Figure 4.2.

Figure 4.2 Click the More button on the interview screen
to get more information when you don't understand a question.

When you click this, you'll see a Tell Me More window that contains more details about the question being asked on the screen. After you've read the explanation in the Tell Me More window, click the OK button to return to the interview.

Choosing an Industry

After you enter your company name and tax ID information, QuickBooks displays a list of industries like the one shown in Figure 4.3.

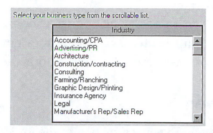

Figure 4.3 The Industry list.

Select an industry from this list that most closely matches your own. When you do this, QuickBooks sets up your chart of accounts to contain some of the typical account names that you'll need for your type of business. (You'll see the account names later in the interview.)

Once you have finished with this subsection, you'll be asked to indicate company preferences such as whether or not you maintain an inventory, whether you want to use time tracking (in QuickBooks Pro), or what sort of invoice format you'd like. The invoice format options are shown in Figure 4.4.

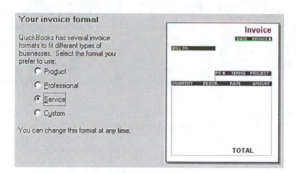

Figure 4.4 You can choose one of four invoice formats during the setup interview.

The sample invoice at the right changes depending on which button you click on the left so you can see how the format you select will actually look. QuickBooks automatically suggests a format that matches the type of industry you previously selected. Since we chose a construction company as our industry type, QuickBooks now recommends the service invoice format.

Note: *Don't worry if the invoice format doesn't look exactly like the one you're using now—you can customize the invoice form later.*

Next, you're asked whether or not you collect sales taxes and then whether you pay one or more sales tax rates.

The final questions in the General section ask you to choose a start date. (See "Setting Your Start Date" in Chapter 3 or "Choosing Conversion and Start Dates" at the beginning of this chapter for more information.)

Income & Expenses

At the beginning of the Income & Expenses section of the interview, you're asked whether you want QuickBooks to set up income and expense account categories for you. We suggest you click the Yes button here. Otherwise, you'll have to go through the tedious process of setting up every account manually.

After you choose an account setup option, you're asked to review and accept the expense accounts QuickBooks has set up as shown in Figure 4.5.

Figure 4.5 The Expense Accounts list lets you review the expense categories that QuickBooks has automatically created for your company.

For now, just click the No button to accept these account categories—you'll fine-tune them later.

Income Details

In the section called Income Details, the Inventory feature is where you specify each inventory item you carry, its sale price, and how many you have in stock. A screen from this part of the interview is shown in Figure 4.6. (If you don't have an inventory, indicate this, and the interview will skip over these questions.)

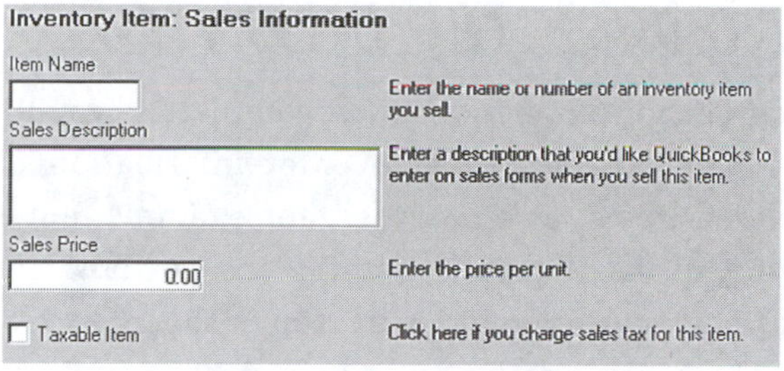

Inventory Item: Sales Information

Item Name

Enter the name or number of an inventory item you sell.

Sales Description

Enter a description that you'd like QuickBooks to enter on sales forms when you sell this item.

Sales Price

0.00

Enter the price per unit.

☐ Taxable Item

Click here if you charge sales tax for this item.

Figure 4.6 The Inventory item form in the setup interview lets you specify the items you sell from stock.

After this, you'll be asked to choose an income account to which you'll apply sales income when you sell this item. A pop-up list contains the names of all the accounts QuickBooks has automatically set up.

Another aspect of this process is supplying inventory purchase information—the item number, description, and cost per unit. When you restock your inventory, you'll write a purchase order telling the vendor his stock number for the item and the cost per unit. Be sure to use the vendor's number for the item, not your own inventory item number!

 Note: *The cost per unit can be changed if your vendor later raises prices. To do this, you use a handy QuickBooks feature called Change Prices, accessed with the Activities menu button at the bottom of your Item list (see "Completing the Item List," later in this chapter).*

Finally, you'll indicate the number of items you have on hand (as of your start date) and the Reorder Point, or the quantity level at which you want QuickBooks to remind you to reorder. When you enter the quantity on hand, QuickBooks multiplies this by the cost per item you entered earlier, then shows you the total value of the items on hand.

You can go through this process for each item in your inventory, if you like. If you have lots of items on hand, though, we suggest you enter only the data for about five or 10 items now to get the hang of it, then do the rest later.

MOVING THROUGH THE INTERVIEW

If you answer each interview question completely, you'll be at it a long time. When it comes time to enter information about customers, vendors, items, or employees, for example, enter data on only a handful of each—just to get the idea of how the process works—and then move on to the next step in the interview. You can add the additional information later as you have time and as new information becomes available. If you have a data-entry clerk, ask the clerk to complete one task (such as entering all customer information) before going on to the next class of information.

Opening Balances

The next part of the interview involves opening balances—the amounts your customers currently owe you and the amounts you currently owe others, plus your checking or savings account balances. Complete this section now, while you're in the interview. Adding your account balances now will make your life easier when you begin using the program for daily transactions. For example, when you receive a payment from a customer, you want QuickBooks to know that you're owed the money so it can properly apply the payment against that customer's outstanding balance.

When you enter a customer balance, you'll type in the customer name and then enter the total that customer owes you, as shown in Figure 4.7.

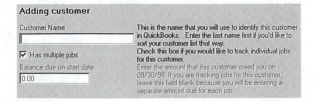

Figure 4.7 The Adding customer screen.

 Tip: *If you have customers for whom you're doing more than one job and you want to track the amounts they owe you on each job, you can indicate that the customer has multiple jobs and then enter each job's name and balance individually on screens that follow.*

After you've added all the customers who owe you money, you'll add vendors to whom you owe money. When entering vendor balances, a lump sum will suffice for each vendor, even if you owe several bills per vendor. (If you're really compulsive, you can go back later and enter the bills separately, but it's not necessary.)

Next, enter your outstanding loans (or liabilities). On each screen, you'll enter the name of a loan account, the unpaid balance as of your start date, and whether or not it's a long-term liability (that is, if it won't be paid off in a year). This gives you the ability to track your outstanding balances, lets QuickBooks remind you when to make payments, and gives you an accurate picture of your business at any time. When you make a loan payment, the unpaid balance of the loan declines and the total interest paid on the loan increases.

When you're done with liability accounts, QuickBooks displays the equity accounts it has automatically created for you (see Figure 4.8).

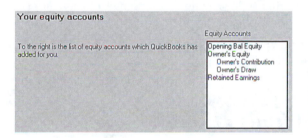

Figure 4.8 You use this part of the interview to review the equity accounts QuickBooks has created for your company.

Your opening balance equity (Opening Bal Equity in Figure 4.8) will be calculated automatically, based on the amounts you enter for the Owner's Equity and Retained Earnings accounts. Owner's Draw is the account you use when you take money out of the business.

Payroll

QuickBooks has a few questions about your payroll, such as what types of payroll taxes and other deductions you withhold for your employees, which ones you are liable for as an employer, and how frequently you pay employees.

Next, you can add the names of your employees to the Employees list. If you don't have many employees, it's easier to enter them all now. The interview makes it very easy to do, as you can see in Figure 4.9.

Figure 4.9 If you don't have many employees, you can add them all to your data file during the interview.

After you finish entering all your employee names and other information, you'll be prompted to enter all the payroll transactions since your start date. Don't do this now—you'll do it after the interview is over.

Finishing the Interview

The rest of the interview is a snap. You can customize the Lists menu by removing items you won't use, for example. You can also display and print some documents that will provide more answers to questions about such things as handling petty cash.

When you're finished with the interview, all the part tabs at the right of the screen should have checkmarks on them.

Reviewing Account Names

Once the interview is complete, QuickBooks has most of the basic information you'll refer to as you enter daily transactions. But before you can begin entering transactions, you must make sure your chart of accounts is complete and that it accurately represents your business.

QuickBooks set up a beginning chart of accounts when you indicated which industry your business was in during the interview, but now it's time to review the account names and edit, delete, or add accounts to track your financial activity more accurately. To view the chart of accounts, choose Lists > Chart of Accounts. You'll see the Chart of Accounts window, which is shown in Figure 4.10.

Name	Type	Balance
◇ Checking	Bank	159.37
◇ Savings	Bank	24,393.42
◇ Accounts Receivable	Accounts Receivable	37,226.83
◇ Employee Loans	Other Current Asset	0.00
◇ Inventory Asset	Other Current Asset	4,113.15
◇ Retainage	Other Current Asset	2,461.80
◇ Undeposited Funds	Other Current Asset	2,124.00
◇ Truck	Fixed Asset	30,750.00
◇ Cost	Fixed Asset	33,750.00
◇ Depreciation	Fixed Asset	-3,000.00
◇ Accounts Payable	Accounts Payable	40,654.20
◇ CalOil Card	Credit Card	71.82
◇ Direct Deposit Liabilities	Other Current Liability	0.00
◇ Payroll Liabilities	Other Current Liability	2,943.60
◇ Sales Tax Payable	Other Current Liability	67.81

Figure 4.10 The Chart of Accounts list.

The best way to set up your chart of accounts accurately is to consult your accountant to make sure you include all the account categories you need. To print out your chart of accounts, choose Lists > Chart of Accounts to display and activate the list, and then choose File > Print List. You can then go over this printed list with your accountant.

Tip: *You can reorder the chart of accounts list by simply selecting an account and dragging it up or down. This allows you to put the accounts you use the most near the top of the list where they're easier to find. You can also drag an account to an indented location below another account to make it a subaccount of that account.*

For more information about setting up accounts, you can also consult the industry-specific document for your type of business (choose Help > QuickBooks and Your Industry) or check out the subtopics under "accounts" in the Help system index.

CASH VERSUS ACCRUAL

QuickBooks can track bills and income in two ways:

- *You can do it on a cash basis (which means that you track income at the time you receive money and expenses at the time when you pay the bills).*

- *You can do it on an accrual basis (which means that you record income at the time of the sale instead of when you receive the payment and expenses when you receive the bill rather than when you pay it).*

If you wish, you can enter your expenses at the time you write checks to pay bills. This is convenient, but it doesn't allow you to take advantage of several money-saving features of QuickBooks. For example, if you enter your bills as you receive them, you can enter the dates when they're due and QuickBooks will remind you to pay them and keep track of the vendors to whom you owe money. Also, if your vendors offer discounts for early payment, QuickBooks allows you to take advantage of this timing. Finally, if you enter your bills as they come in, you can pay them all at once and print all the checks at once. We think this makes sense, especially if you pay a lot of bills each week or month.

Entering Historical Transactions

During the interview, you entered the amounts you owe other people and the amounts your customers owe you. Now you'll need to enter all the actual expense and income transactions you've made from your start date to today. Enter the following in the order shown:

1. Invoices you've sent out since your start date.

2. Purchase orders you've issued since your start date.

3. Cash or checks you've received since your start date.

4. Bills you've received since your start date.

5. Bills you've paid since your start date.

6. Deposits you've made to any of your accounts since your start date.

7. Any other checks you've written (for things other than bills) since your start date.

The order is important because invoices are linked to customer payments and your vendors' bills are linked to purchase orders or payments you make. For example, QuickBooks won't know how to credit a customer payment unless you've previously recorded the invoice to that customer.

We'll offer more details about entering expense and income transactions beginning in Chapter 6, "Daily Activities," but let's look at the basic procedure here.

DO YOUR CHECKBOOK LAST

When entering historical transactions, start with outstanding bills, deposits made since your start date, payments you've received since your start date, and payroll checks you've written. Leave your actual checking account records for last because as you enter the other transactions, they're automatically included in your QuickBooks checking account register. By the time you enter all your historical transactions, your check register will be mostly complete.

Entering a Customer Payment

To enter a payment you've received from a customer, follow these steps:

1. Choose Activities > Receive Payments. You'll see a form like the one shown in Figure 4.11.

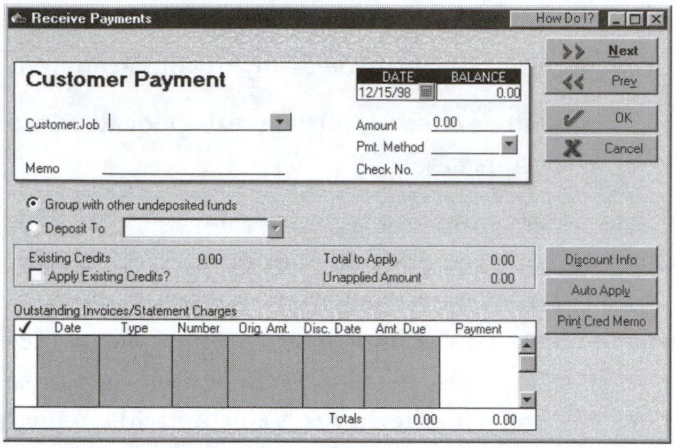

Figure 4.11 The Receive Payments form.

2. Type the customer's name, or choose it from the pop-up list. Quick-Books will show the outstanding balance for this customer in the Balance box at the right and any outstanding invoices for this customer will be listed in the detail area at the bottom.

3. Enter the date of the transaction (you're entering historical transactions right now so you'll have to change the date because QuickBooks automatically suggests today's date).

4. Enter the amount of the payment.

5. Choose a payment method from the pop-up list next to the Pmt. Method blank.

6. Fill in the information about the check number and the account to which you'll deposit the funds.

7. Click in the checkmark column next to the invoice(s) to which you want to apply this payment in the detail area.

8. Click the OK button to record the transaction or click the Next button to record this transaction and display a new form.

Tip: *When you're entering income transactions, enter your sales, payments from sales, and deposits of those payments in the order that they occurred. These transactions must have accurate dates as well. If you enter reference numbers from your sales slips and invoices, QuickBooks will keep track of these numbers in order and will assign new numbers consecutively.*

Entering a Bill You've Received

Here are the steps you would follow to record a bill you've received but haven't yet paid:

1. Choose Enter Bills from the Activities menu. You'll see the Enter Bills form, which is shown in Figure 4.12.

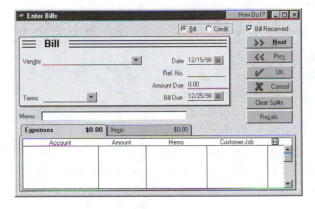

Figure 4.12
The Enter Bills form.

2. Type the vendor name or choose it from the pop-up list.

3. Type in the date you received the bill and a reference number, if any, from the bill.

4. Type in the amount due, and then type in the terms of the bill or choose an option from the pop-up list.

5. Type in the date the bill is due.

6. Click the Expenses or Items tab in the detail area, then enter the data about the type of expense or item you're buying.

Note: You can split a bill transaction, assigning parts of it to different jobs if you wish. See "Splitting Transactions" in Chapter 6 for details.

7. Click the OK or Next button to record the data.

ENTER TRANSACTIONS IN ORDER

When you're entering expense transactions, enter bills paid and credit card charges you've made in the order that they occurred, with the correct date. Each new transaction form will default to today's date, so be sure to enter the correct date manually. You must be accurate because QuickBooks is very sensitive to date information. (For example, you can't enter income for a bill collected on a date that precedes the invoice for the same bill.) QuickBooks also assigns purchase order numbers and invoice numbers automatically, in sequence.

As you enter these items, they'll automatically be added to your checking account register.

This brief summary should give you an idea of how to perform these activities. For more information, see Chapter 6, "Daily Activities."

Bringing Your Payroll Up to Date

Now you must enter all your payroll expenses (paycheck information) from January 1 to your start date.

1. Choose Activities > Payroll > Set Up YTD Amounts. You'll see the Set Up YTD Amounts wizard, which is shown in Figure 4.13.

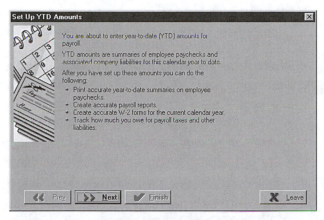

Figure 4.13 The Set Up YTD Amounts wizard.

2. Read the opening screen carefully and make sure you have the information you'll need at hand.

3. Enter the data as indicated and click Next to work your way through this wizard. Some of your answers will depend on how you kept payroll records in the past and the length of time between your start date and the beginning of the year.

4. When you reach the list of employees, select each employee name in turn and click the Enter Summary button. You'll see a form like the one shown in Figure 4.14.

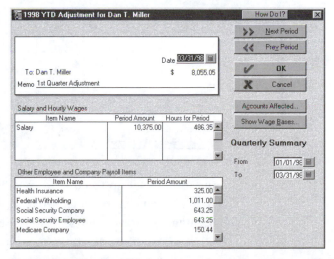

Figure 4.14 Use the YTD Adjustment form to enter the year's historical pay data for each employee.

5. Enter the total wages or salary, hours, and other payroll costs in the appropriate blanks in the Salary and Hourly Wages detail area.

 Note: The Accounts Affected button at the right lets you assign the wages and other payroll costs to specific liability or bank accounts. For example, you might want to assign one employee's payroll costs to a liability account called Labor and another's wage costs to an account called Supervision.

6. Click the Next Period button to store the next quarter's data for this employee and repeat step 5.

7. Click the OK button. You'll be returned to the Employee YTD Adjustments dialog box and you can then select the next employee on the list and repeat the process.

8. When you've entered all the historical payroll information for every employee you'll be returned to the Set Up YTD Amounts dialog box. Click the Next button. You'll be asked if you want to enter prior tax and other payroll liability payments you've made during the year.

9. Click the Create button. You'll see the Prior Payment of Taxes and Liabilities form, which is shown in Figure 4.15.

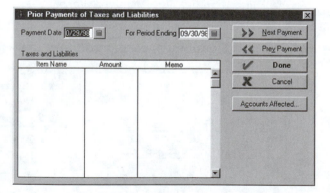

Figure 4.15
The Prior Payment of Taxes and Liabilities form.

10. Notice that the form is set up to cover a specific quarterly period. Click in the Item Name column. You'll see a pop-up list of standard payroll liability items you can choose. Enter your prior payroll liability information, one account at a time (payroll tax, social security,

and so on). To assign these costs to specific liability accounts, click the Accounts Affected button and choose the account(s) from the list there.

11. If you made several payments in different months or quarters, click the Next Payment button and enter data on the payment or group of payments for the next quarter.

12. Click the OK button when you've entered all the paid liabilities and you're done.

By entering this information, you'll ensure that QuickBooks has complete payroll records for the year, and that you'll be able to file your taxes easily and accurately. For information about handling your weekly payroll, see "Preparing a Payroll" in Chapter 7.

WHAT ABOUT NON-EMPLOYEE COMPENSATION?

If you know you'll be paying daily contractors, consultants, or others who aren't on the payroll, you should set them up as vendors who will receive 1099 forms at the end of the year. Add each consultant or contractor as a new vendor to your Vendors list, click the Additional Information tab, and then check the Vendor Eligible for 1099 checkbox. You can also identify specific item accounts (Computer Consulting, for example) with 1099 payments. For more information, see "Preparing 1099-MISC forms" in Chapter 10.

Bank Account Information

If you entered all your historical transactions, your checking account or savings account register already contains lots of entries reflecting bills you've paid, checks you've written for other purposes, and deposits you've received. But there are other transactions that you must now enter in order to make your account registers complete:

- Checks or other charges that happened before your start date but didn't appear on statements before your start date.

- Other checks you wrote after your start date that were not for bills or accounts payable (credit card payments, for example).

- Deposits made after your start date that were not customer payments.

- Deposits you made before your start date that didn't appear on statements before your start date.

- Bank charges and fees.

- Interest paid on your account.

To add these items to your account, you could enter them individually by writing checks or making deposits, but the simplest way is to enter them directly into your account register. Every account listed in your chart of accounts has its own register.

1. Choose Lists > Chart of Accounts to display the Chart of Accounts list.

2. Double-click the name of the checking or savings account you want to debit or credit to display its register. You'll see a sample register in Figure 4.16.

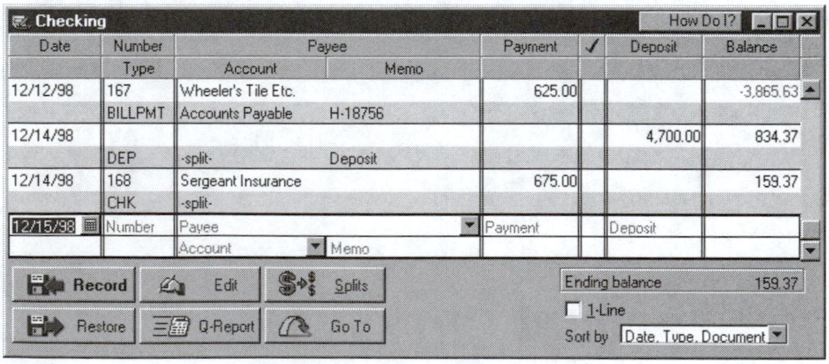

Figure 4.16 The Checking account register.

3. Click in the blank row at the bottom of the register.

4. Enter the transaction data as explained under "Entering Data into a Register" in Chapter 1.

5. Click the Record button to record the transaction.

6. Repeat this procedure for the next transaction in the blank row that appears below the one you just filled out.

Note: *You can split transactions by assigning different portions of a check or deposit to different accounts. See "Splitting Transactions" in Chapter 6 for more information.*

Completing Customer and Vendor Data

During the interview, you probably entered data on only a few customers and vendors. Now it's time to enter the rest.

To enter data on a new customer, follow these steps:

1. Choose Lists > Customers:Jobs. You'll see the Customer:Job List list shown in Figure 4.17.

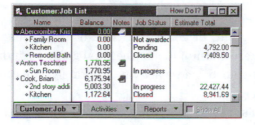

Figure 4.17 The Customer:Job list.

2. Click the right mouse button and then select New. You'll see a New Customer form.

3. Fill in the customer information and then click the Next button to add another new customer, or click the OK button to enter the data and put away the New Customer dialog box.

Tip: *To add a new job for an existing customer, select the customer's name in the Customer:Job list, click the right mouse button, and choose Add Job from the pop-up menu.*

The procedure is very similar when you enter data on a new vendor. Choose Lists > Vendors to display the Vendor list. Click the right mouse button and choose New from the pop-up menu and you'll see a New Vendor form where you can enter the new vendor data.

Enter Vendors and Customers with Balances First

When you enter vendor information, enter those to whom you owe money first. The same goes for customers—enter the ones who owe you money first. This way, QuickBooks will automatically credit your accounts for vendors or customers when you enter payments or pay bills. If you try to enter a payment from a customer before entering the bill you sent that customer, QuickBooks won't apply the payment against the invoice; instead, it will offer to issue a credit memo to the customer.

Completing the Item List

Items are categories of goods, services, or other things you buy or sell. QuickBooks starts a list of items when you go through the interview, but in order to track your business activity accurately, you'll want to add to this list considerably.

The Item list can be somewhat complicated because items can be anything from inventory items to sales tax, subtotals, or discounts. Once you begin adding items, though, you'll find the process goes pretty smoothly.

Choosing Items for Your Business

Businesses that sell unique items, such as paintings or real estate, shouldn't list each item separately in QuickBooks. Items should be used to designate groups of items, or items that you sell repeatedly from inventory. See Appendix B, "Customizing QuickBooks for Your Business," for advice about setting up items for your business, or refer to the QuickBooks and Your Industry documents on the Help menu for more information.

Let's start by looking at the item list. Choose Lists > Items. You'll see the Item List window shown in Figure 4.18.

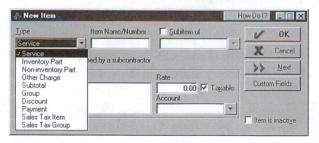

Figure 4.18
The Item List.

As you can see, items have names, descriptions, types, accounts to which they must be applied, prices (or tax or discount rates), and quantities on hand (if you're tracking inventory). This list has inventory items on it because it includes sample data. Now you must fill out your own company's Item list.

The information you supply when adding new items depends on the type of item you're describing. Here's how the process works:

1. Click the right mouse button and then choose New from the pop-up menu. You'll see a New Item form as shown in Figure 4.19.

Figure 4.19
The New Item form.

2. Choose the type of item you want to add from the pop-up list in the upper-left corner. There are several item types; choose the one that best fits the item you're entering.

Tip: *If you're not sure what type to assign to different items, check the sample company data to see how it's done there or look at one of the subtopics under "items" in the Help system index.*

After you choose an item type, the rest of the New Item form can change, depending on the item type you chose. The example above shows the information blanks for a Service item, but some items require more information than this. Figure 4.20, for example, shows the data-entry blanks when you've chosen an Inventory Part item.

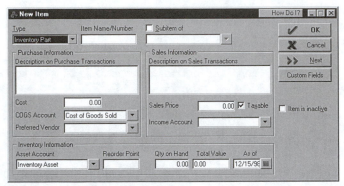

Figure 4.20 When you add inventory items, the New Item form collects additional information.

In this case, you must supply two descriptions of the item—Purchase Information that refers to it as the item's vendor does (for use on purchase orders, for example), and Sales Information that refers to it as you do when selling it (for use on invoices, for example).

You also need to enter three different accounts for the item: a COGS (Cost of Goods Sold) Account to identify the item when you buy it; an Income Account to identify the item when you sell it; and an Asset Account item to identify the item as an inventory asset.

Tip: *If you fill in the Cost and Quantity on Hand blanks for an Inventory Part item, QuickBooks will automatically calculate the value of the items on hand and enter it in the Total Value box.*

For more information about how to choose the right account for an item, see "accounts" in the Help system index.

By the time you've finished all the activities in this chapter, your QuickBooks system will be set up and ready to go to work, tracking your daily, weekly, and monthly transactions as they occur. In Chapter 6, "Daily Activities" and Chapter 7, "Weekly and Monthly Activities," you'll see how to do just that.

CUSTOMIZING AND UPDATING QUICKBOOKS

We all have our own ideas about how our business forms and records should look, how QuickBooks collects data, and how the program should conform to our working style. In this chapter, you'll see how to use preferences, passwords, and custom templates to precisely tailor QuickBooks forms and data-handling options for your business. You'll also see how to update your copy of the QuickBooks program and update your program's tax tables.

If you're looking for information about customizing reports, see "Customizing a Report" in Chapter 8.

Setting Preferences

QuickBooks has dozens of preferences you can set to change the way the program works. You can set preferences for accounting methods, check writing, finance charges, payroll, sales, sales tax, vendors, taxes, time tracking, and other aspects of your accounting operation. Most of these preferences will be customized for your business as you work through the interview process, but you can reset them at any time.

About User and Company Preferences

Since QuickBooks version 6 can be set up for access by several different users, you can create individual user names and passwords to grant access to the program for different employees. (See "Creating User Names and Passwords" later in this chapter.)

The QuickBooks Preferences dialog box allows you to set preferences for yourself, the user who is currently logged into QuickBooks (if you have set up additional users), or for the entire company. There are two types of preferences you can set:

- **User preferences** are specific settings that cover the way information is displayed, such as how reports are formatted, whether or not QCards appear on the screen, which buttons appear in the Iconbar, and which commands appear on the Lists and Activities menus.

- **Company preferences** control how accounting information is processed throughout the program for all users. For example, you can set options to control how QuickBooks handles data related to payroll, sales, purchases, taxes, time tracking, and finance charges.

 Note: *If you set up additional users for your company file in Quick-Books, you must open your company file using the administrator's password in order to access or change company preferences. Only the administrator has permission to change these options. If you are the only user of QuickBooks Pro, you have access to the company preferences automatically. For more information about users and the QuickBooks administrator, see "Creating User Names and Passwords," later in this chapter.*

Using the Preferences Dialog Box

All preferences options are controlled through the Preferences dialog box. To access and set preferences options:

1. Choose File > Preferences. You'll see the Preferences dialog box shown in Figure 5.1.

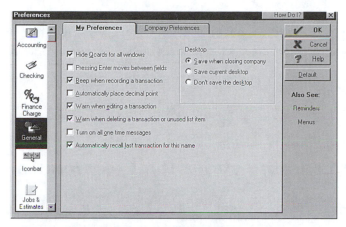

Figure 5.1 The Preferences dialog box lets you set a variety of custom options in QuickBooks.

The preferences are divided into 15 different categories represented by the icons in the scrolling list at the left. You'll also notice the My Preferences and Company Preferences tabs at the top of the options area.

2. Click an icon to display its group of preferences. The My Preferences tab is automatically selected so you can select preferences for yourself as an individual user.

3. Click the Company Preferences tab to set preferences that affect all users of the program.

Note: *Most of the preferences categories are for options related to data handling so there are no options on the My Preferences tab for these categories.*

4. Select the personal or company preferences you want using the pop-up lists, checkboxes, radio buttons, and data boxes in the right side of the dialog box.

Tip: *The Also See area below the buttons at the right side of the Preferences dialog box suggests other categories of preferences that are related to the ones you're currently viewing.*

5. Click another icon at the left to display more preferences, if you like. You'll be asked if you want to save the changes you just made. Click OK to set the new group of options.

6. Repeat steps 2–5 to set other options, if you like.

7. Click the OK button to store the changes you made and put away the dialog box.

Learning about the Preferences

Many of the preferences cover fairly technical aspects of accounting and you may not understand them right away. To find out about the preferences you're viewing, click the Help button at the right side of the dialog box. You'll see a list of topics that matches the name of each preference in the category you are viewing and you can simply click on any topic to find out exactly what that preference does. As an alternative, click the How Do I? button at the top of the Preferences dialog box and choose a Help topic from the pop-up menu.

Restoring Default Preferences

If you ever decide you don't like the custom preferences you've set for one or more categories, you can return them to the standard QuickBooks options. Just choose File > Preferences, click the icon for the category you want to reset, click the tab for user or company preferences, and then click the Default button at the right.

Creating User Names and Passwords

Multiple users at a company can use QuickBooks. If you set up more than one user for your QuickBooks installation, you'll be asked to log on with a user name and password each time you start the program. Passwords allow you to prevent unauthorized users from seeing, adding, changing, or printing different types of data in your company file.

When you begin using QuickBooks, the program assigns the first user name, "Admin," to you. You can keep this name or change it and you can add a password to it for more security. If you're the only person using

QuickBooks, your user name and password will prevent anyone else from opening your company data file. It's not necessary for you or any other user to have a password, but we think it's a good idea.

If more than one person will access your QuickBooks data file, user names and passwords will allow you to control each user's access in a very precise way.

Setting Your Own Password

To set a password for yourself:

1. Choose File > Set Up Users and Passwords > Set Up Users. You'll see the Set Up QuickBooks Administrator dialog box shown in Figure 5.2.

Figure 5.2 The first time you create a user name and password, you must set up the administrator name and password.

QuickBooks automatically lists your user name as "Admin" because in multiuser situations it requires one user to be the QuickBooks administrator. The QuickBooks administrator is the only person who has the ability to add or change other user names or passwords, or to set company preferences.

2. If you don't like the user name "Admin," type a different name in the Administrator's Name box.

3. Press the Tab key and type a password in the Administrator's Password box. Choose a password that will be easy for you to remember but hard for others to guess. Combinations of numbers and letters work best.

4. Press the Tab key again and type the same password in the Confirm Password box.

5. Click the OK button to save your password. After this, you'll be asked to enter your password each time you open your company data file.

Adding Other Users and Passwords

If your company data file will be used by more than one person, you should assign each person a user name and password. Then, when each user logs on when opening your company data file, that user can set his or her own "My Preferences" options as described earlier in this chapter under "Using the Preferences Dialog Box."

To add other user names and passwords:

1. Choose File > Set Up Users and Passwords > Set Up Users. You'll see the User List dialog box shown in Figure 5.3.

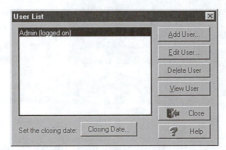

Figure 5.3 As the QuickBooks administrator, you can create new users or see who is logged on at any time.

Click the Add User button. You'll see the User Name and Password wizard shown in Figure 5.4.

Figure 5.4 The User Name and Password wizard walks you through the process of assigning user access privileges.

2. Type a user name in the User Name box then enter the user's password in the Password and Confirm Password boxes below.

3. Click the Next button. You'll see a series of screens where you can permit or deny access to various parts of QuickBooks, such as accounts receivable, accounts payable, checking accounts, time-tracking activities, financial reports, and changing or deleting transactions. On each screen, you can allow full access or choose selective access, such as allowing the user to create transactions but not print them. Click the Next button as you choose options on each screen.

4. When you're finished setting the user's options, you'll see a screen that summarizes them. Click the Previous button to reset a group of privileges from a prior screen if necessary.

5. Click the Finish button to store the privileges and return to the User List dialog box.

Viewing, Changing, and Deleting a User's Privileges

You can review any user's privileges with the User List dialog box as well.

1. Choose File > Set Up Users and Passwords > Set Up Users to display the User List dialog box.

2. Select the user name in the dialog box.

3. Click the View User button. You'll see a list of the user's specific access privileges.

To change a user's privileges, select the user name in the User List dialog box and click the Edit User button. You'll see the User Name and Password wizard again, and you can reset the user's privileges in the same way that you created them in the first place.

To delete a user, select the user name in the User List dialog box and click the Delete User button.

Customizing Form Templates

The standard forms you see in QuickBooks are more than adequate for common business procedures and you can choose from a variety of pre-designed templates to suit most situations. However, if you want to include other types of data not shown on the pre-designed form templates, you can customize them.

 Note: *Not all forms can be customized. If you don't see the Custom Template list on a form, that form can't be customized.*

Selecting a Pre-designed Template

QuickBooks comes with several pre-designed templates. If you don't like the default form that appears when you perform an activity, just select a different one from the Custom Template pop-up list at the top right corner of the form. See Figure 5.5.

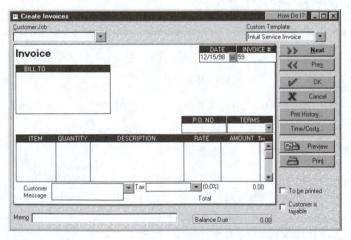

Figure 5.5
The Custom Template pop-up list appears in the upper-right corner of forms that can be customized.

 Tip: *The Custom Template pop-up list shows only the templates for the type of form you're using. To see all of the templates included in QuickBooks, choose Lists > Templates.*

Customizing a Pre-designed Template

The easiest way to customize a template is to change an existing one that's already close to the way you want it.

1. Open the form whose template you want to customize then choose the template you want to change from the Custom Templates pop-up list, if necessary, to display it.

 Tip: *You can also select a template by choosing Lists > Templates, selecting the template in the list, and choosing Edit with the Templates menu button.*

2. Choose Customize from the top of the Custom Templates list. You'll see the Customize Template dialog box shown in Figure 5.6.

Figure 5.6 The Customize Template dialog box lets you select a template to customize or create a new one.

3. Click the Edit button or the New button. You'll see the Customize Invoice dialog box shown in Figure 5.7.

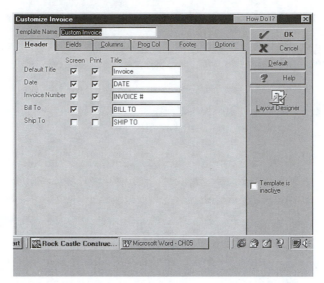

Figure 5.7 Once you select an invoice to customize, you'll have lots of options for changing it.

4. The Customize Invoice dialog box mainly allows you to add or remove data or labels from a form. Click the tabs at the top of this dialog box to display different sets of options then select the options you want on each tab.

Note: *If you selected a template whose name starts with "Intuit" in Step 1, you will only see the Options tab in the Customize dialog box.*

5. Click the Layout Designer and use it to rearrange information on the invoice, if you like. (See "Using the Layout Designer" next for details.)

6. To save the template with a different name, enter a new name in the Template Name box.

7. Click OK to save the change. If you changed the invoice name, the new name will appear on the Custom Templates list.

Tip: For more information about any of the options in the Customize dialog box, click the tab whose options you want to know about and then click the Help button.

Using the Layout Designer

The Customize dialog box offers point-and-click options for changing the contents of a form, but it won't let you rearrange the contents. When you want to move the data boxes on a template, reset the font or alignment of text in one or more specific data boxes, or resize columns or boxes in a precise way, you can use the Layout Designer.

To open the Layout Designer, display the Customize dialog box (page 101), then click the Layout Designer button. The Layout Designer window is shown in Figure 5.8.

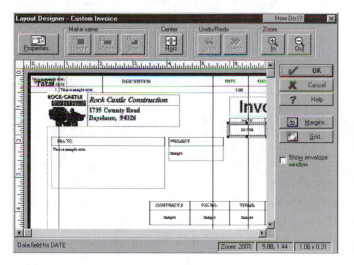

Figure 5.8
In the Layout Designer window, you can move or resize fields and perform other detailed modifications to templates

Note: You can't use the Layout Designer when you're editing one of the Intuit-named templates.

Essentially, the Layout Designer is a drawing program that lets you select any text, line, box, or colored area on a template and move it or change its appearance in other ways. You can select and move objects by clicking and dragging inside the form itself, or you can perform other operations with the buttons at the top and side of the form.

Tip: *Double-click on a field or field label to change its text or border options.*

To learn more about the Layout Designer program, click the Help button in the Layout Designer dialog box and then select a topic inside the Help window.

What You Can't Do with the Layout Designer

You have a lot of flexibility with the Layout Designer, but there are limits. You can't:

- *Delete or rename any field. Use the Fields options in the Customize dialog box to rename or eliminate fields.*

- *Change the paper size for forms. Choose File > Printer Setup, choose the form type from the pop-up list, then click the Options button to change these options.*

Using the Templates List Window

When you use the Templates list window, you have several additional options for managing templates. To use these options, choose Lists > Templates, select a template in the list that appears, click the Templates menu button at the bottom of the window, and choose a command. Here's a quick rundown of some key template management activities you can perform.

Deleting or Duplicating a Template

You can delete a template by selecting it in the Templates list and choosing Delete with the Templates menu button. To duplicate a template, select it and choose the Duplicate command with the Templates menu button—the duplicate will appear in the list with the name "DUP" followed by the name of the original.

Making a Template Inactive

If you have lots of templates and there are some that you don't use frequently, you can make them inactive. Inactive templates are still stored in your QuickBooks data file, but they don't appear in the Templates list window or on the Custom Template pop-up list.

To make a template inactive, select it in the Templates list window and choose Make Inactive with the Templates menu button.

To reactivate a template, choose Show All Templates using the Templates menu button, select the inactive template in the Templates list (it will have a ghost icon next to it), and choose Make Active with the Templates menu button.

Importing and Exporting Templates

If you created a really great custom template in another QuickBooks data file and you want to use it in your current data file, or you want to share one of your templates with another QuickBooks user, you can import or export the template.

To export a template, select it in the Templates list window, choose the Export command with the Templates menu button, then save the template file. Try to use a name that clearly identifies the template's purpose.

To import a template, choose Import with the Templates menu button, then navigate to the template file you want and open it.

Selecting a Default Template

When you create an invoice, estimate, or other form that uses templates, QuickBooks always uses the same default template each time you display that form. You can select a different default template if you like. Just select the template name and choose the Use command with the Templates menu button. You don't need to have a form open to use this command—the next time you open that template's type of form (invoice, statement, and so on), the template you selected for use will be showing.

Updating QuickBooks

Periodically, Intuit offers updates, or "maintenance releases," of the current version of QuickBooks that fix bugs or enhance the program's performance. These updates are free to registered owners of QuickBooks and you can download them from an Intuit Web site. If you have subscribed to Intuit's tax table update service, you can also update your tax table.

Updating the QuickBooks Program

To get a free update of your program (or see if one is available):

1. Choose Online > QuickBooks Update Service. You'll see the Quick-Books Update Service dialog box shown in Figure 5.9.

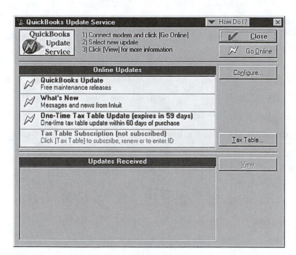

Figure 5.9 You can use the QuickBooks Update Service to receive program updates, tax table updates, or messages from Intuit via the World Wide Web.

2. Click the Go Online button. QuickBooks will launch your Web browser, navigate to the QuickBooks update Web site, download the latest version of QuickBooks, and then sign off. You'll see a message in the New Updates list that explains which items were downloaded.

Note: *You need a modem and an Internet access account to use any of the QuickBooks online services. If you haven't yet set up QuickBooks to access resources on the Internet, you'll be asked to do so when updating. See "Using Online Features in QuickBooks" in Chapter 1.*

3. Select an item in the Updates Received list and click the View button for a description of the update you received or to read a message from Intuit, if you received one.

4. Click the Close button. If you received a program update, your copy of the QuickBooks program will be updated automatically.

Updating Your Tax Tables

You can also use the QuickBooks Update Service dialog box to sign up for a one-year subscription to Intuit's monthly tax table updates. Just choose Online > QuickBooks Update Service then click the Tax Tables button in the QuickBooks Update Service dialog box. QuickBooks will launch your Web browser and connect you to the tax table update service where you can read about what it offers and subscribe online. Once you sign up for the service, you can receive new updates by choosing Online > Payroll Tax Tables.

PART II

RUNNING YOUR BUSINESS WITH QUICKBOOKS

DAILY ACTIVITIES

The bread and butter of your QuickBooks accounting system is the data about your daily and weekly financial activities. These activities include income-producing tasks such as making cash sales, receiving payments, making deposits, tracking time, and creating invoices; and expense-related activities such as creating purchase orders, paying bills, writing checks, and preparing a payroll.

In this chapter, we'll look at the daily activities along with activities you can perform any day (rather than those you perform on a fixed schedule). We'll cover regularly scheduled weekly and monthly activities in Chapter 7, "Weekly and Monthly Activities."

Before we explore the daily activities, let's consider the big picture: how and when to capture your accounting data.

Capturing Your Accounting Data

Everyone in business has a million things to do besides worrying about accounting, but your QuickBooks system (like any accounting system) relies on the timely and accurate capture of essential accounting facts. To make the most of QuickBooks, you'll have to work data-capturing into your daily business life. Capturing data includes every accounting activity, whether it's writing a check, preparing an invoice, or logging an employee's time.

THE DATA CAPTURE ORDER MATTERS

Whatever your schedule is for handling accounting chores, enter outstanding bills and time data before you prepare invoices and payroll. This makes your life easier for several reasons:

- *Recording bills and time data before you invoice makes invoicing much easier because time and material cost information is already stored and can easily be added to each invoice.*

- *Recording time data daily or weekly makes preparing your payroll much easier because employee time for each period is already recorded.*

- *Recording your outstanding bills as you receive them makes check writing easier because you can have QuickBooks automatically write checks for outstanding bills you've previously recorded.*

Your challenge is to integrate the collection of accounting data seamlessly into your daily operations. To do this, you might set aside a half-hour or so every day to make the entries yourself—right after closing time, perhaps. If you're using QuickBooks with multiple users, you may have one or more people handling accounting chores throughout the day. If you're in a retail business, you may have QuickBooks set up on a computer at the point of sale so your sales clerks can capture the data as each sale is made.

However you capture data, though, think of QuickBooks as a system of interlocking functions, and keep in mind that some of those functions affect others. For example, when you receive a customer payment, QuickBooks looks up all the previously unpaid invoices for that customer so you can easily credit the payment against them. If you haven't yet created invoices for the customer, you have to do some extra work to credit the payment properly.

To use QuickBooks most efficiently, it's important to capture your accounting data regularly and in the proper order. When you capture expense and income data every day, for example, QuickBooks automatically supplies the correct transaction date and you'll have a much better chance of remembering small details about each transaction than if you're trying to record them a week after the fact. Recording data frequently also means you'll always have up-to-date information for QuickBooks reports on the health of your business. Finally, collecting data frequently is easier than doing weekly sessions because there's less data to enter in a single sitting.

Here's a suggested schedule for capturing different types of data with QuickBooks:

- **Cash sales.** Record these the day you make them.

- **Bills you receive.** Enter these the day you get them. If you're buying inventory items, enter the amount you paid each item. If you're buying a service or item for a particular customer, include the customer's name in the bill detail.

- **Inventory you receive.** Enter receipts of inventory items the day you get them so your on-hand inventory levels are current and the information is available when you create invoices.

- **Checks you write.** Enter these the day you write them and code items you buy with them for a particular customer, if necessary.

- **Payments you receive.** Record these the day you receive them so your accounts receivable are always up to date.

- **Deposits.** These are usually made daily (for cash-based businesses) or weekly.

- **Time data.** If you charge customers for time, enter the time data daily or at least make sure that you've entered all the time data for a particular billing period before you create an invoice for that customer. If your business is a consulting firm that bills by the hour or fractions of hours and you're using QuickBooks Pro, distribute the QuickBooks Pro Timer program and ask each employee to send you weekly or biweekly timer files. (See "Using the QuickBooks Pro Timer" later in this chapter.)

- **Invoices.** We'll assume you invoice once a week. If you invoice more frequently, make sure you've entered all the expense information you need first. If you're recording expenses for items you sell to customers (along with any payments you receive) every day, your invoices and accounts receivable figures will always be accurate. (See Chapter 7, "Weekly and Monthly Activities," for more on invoicing.)

- **Payroll.** Prepare your payroll one or two days after the close of a pay period to allow for possible adjustments to time figures you've collected during the period. (See Chapter 7 for details.)

- **Purchase orders.** You can prepare these at any time, but if you're buying items for which you hope to bill customers immediately, create them before you prepare invoices. (See Chapter 7 for details.)

- **Estimates.** Prepare these any time (see "Making Estimates," later in this chapter). You can turn the estimate into an invoice and bill for the whole project or by a percentage of completion. (See "Invoicing for Work in Progress" in Chapter 7.)

Let's take a closer look at each of these activities.

Making Cash Sales

You can make cash sales to anonymous buyers or you can store new customer information when filling out the Enter Cash Sales form. (If you have a retail business, you probably won't have nearly enough time to record every customer's name and address unless you sell small quantities of expensive items, such as Bentleys or Ferraris.) The Enter Cash Sales form allows you to enter sales by cash, check, or credit card and to print a receipt for the customer if you wish. You can also use this form instead of the Receive Payments form (see "Receiving Payments," later in this chapter) if a customer hands you a check rather than waiting for you to send an invoice.

 Note: *QuickBooks lets you store up to 14,500 Customer, Vendor, Employee, and Other Names all together. Store information only for customers who will be repeaters.*

When you record cash sales, they are stored as income in the account you have designated for income from sales. Each sale is assigned to the item(s) listed in the detail area of the Enter Cash Sales form so you know how many of what items you sold. QuickBooks also depletes your inventory to account for the items sold.

The Enter Cash Sales Form

To store a cash sale:

1. Choose Activities > Enter Cash Sales. You'll see a form like the one shown in Figure 6.1.

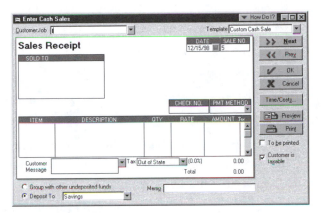

Figure 6.1 The Enter Cash Sales form.

2. QuickBooks will automatically enter today's date and a sale number in the form. Change them if necessary.

3. If the sale is to an existing customer, type the customer's last name in the Customer:Job box or choose the name from the pop-up list. QuickBooks will fill in the Sold To box and automatically select the customer's tax status (the Customer is taxable checkbox) at the lower-right corner of the form.

 Tip: *If you're entering a cash sale to a one-time customer, leave the Customer:Job box empty. If you type in a new name, QuickBooks will force you to add the new customer's information to your Customers list. If the customer wants his or her name on the receipt, type it in the Sold To box.*

4. If you're tracking income by class, choose a class from the Class pop-up list at the top of the form.

5. If the customer is paying by check, click in the Check No. box and enter the check number.

6. Choose a payment method from the pop-up list in the PMT Method box.

7. Press Tab to move the cursor to the top line of the Item column in the detail area. If you've sold an item that's stored in your Items list (see "Completing the Item List" in Chapter 4) choose its name from the pop-up list in the Item column and the item description will automatically be filled in.

8. Press Tab to move the cursor to the Description column and type a brief description.

9. Press Tab to move the cursor to the QTY column and enter the number of items sold.

10. Press Tab and enter the Rate information (unit cost or hourly labor rate) in the Rate column. QuickBooks will automatically calculate the figure in the Amount column.

11. Press Tab again to move to the next blank line in the detail area if you want to enter another item, or just click in a blank line in any of the columns.

12. If the sale is taxable, make sure the Customer is Taxable checkbox is checked at the right side of the form and verify the tax rate in the Tax box or choose a different one from the pop-up list.

13. The Group with Other Undeposited Funds button is usually selected. It tells QuickBooks to add the amount of this sale to a deposit slip the next time you make up one for the bank. If you are rushing off to the bank immediately after this sale and you want to record the sale as having been deposited, click the Deposit To checkbox and choose the name of the bank from the pop-up list.

14. Click the OK, Next, or Prev button to store the transaction.

 Note: *You can also press the Enter key to store any transaction. Never press the Enter key to move from one line to the next in a data blank (the Sold To area, for example), because you'll store the transaction. This caution holds true for every transaction form in QuickBooks.*

WHAT ABOUT PENDING TRANSACTIONS?

When a sale is under way but hasn't been officially completed, you can mark a sales receipt or invoice as pending by choosing Edit > Mark Cash Sale as Pending or Edit > Mark Invoice as Pending. This will record the transaction, but the transaction won't be added to your account ledgers until you tell QuickBooks the sale is final. You can do the same thing with credit memos; see "pending sales" in the Help system index.

Printing Cash Receipts

You can print a cash sale receipt directly from the Enter Cash Sales form or you can add receipts to a batch and then print them all at once later. To print the form immediately, click the Print button then select printing options in the Print dialog box.

To indicate that you'd like to print the receipt later, check the "To be printed" checkbox in the lower-right corner. Then, when you want to print a batch of receipts at a later time:

1. Choose File > Print Forms > Print Sales Receipts. You'll see the Select Receipts to Print dialog box shown in Figure 6.2.

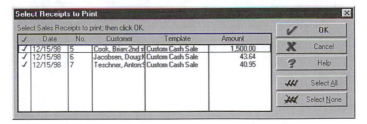

Figure 6.2 The Select Receipts to Print dialog box.

2. The list shows all the receipts you have scheduled for printing. Click the Select All button to select all receipts for printing or click in the checkmark column to select individual receipts.

3. Click the Print button, select printing options, and then click OK to print the receipts.

Recording Bills Received

If you record bills and payment due dates as soon as you receive them, QuickBooks will remind you when they're due, and you'll always know exactly how much you owe. When you enter a bill, you enter the total amount and the date the bill is due, along with the specific items (usually goods) or expenses (usually services) that the bill is for. This way, QuickBooks keeps track of your total expenses for each specific item or expense.

The basic procedure for entering bills you receive was covered in "Entering a Bill You've Received" in Chapter 4. Now, let's look more closely at the options you have when doing this.

The Enter Bills Form

When you choose Activities > Enter Bills, you will see a form like the one shown in Figure 6.3.

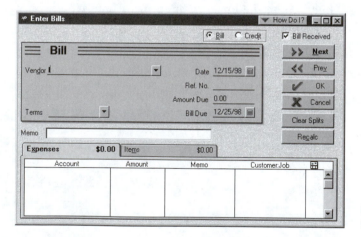

Figure 6.3 The Enter Bills form.

The upper part of the form says who the bill is from and how much it is, and the lower portion contains details about the items or services purchased.

Tip: *You can also use the Enter Bills form to record credit memos from vendors. Click the Credit button at the top of the form to record a credit memo rather than a bill. To record an expense for which you haven't yet received a bill, uncheck the Bill Received checkbox at the upper-right corner.*

If you're entering a bill from a new vendor whose information you haven't previously stored on your Vendors list, type the vendor's full name and then press Tab. QuickBooks will tell you it can't find the vendor's record and will give you a chance to add it (see Figure 6.4).

Figure 6.4 When you try to use a new customer name, QuickBooks asks you to add it to your Customers list.

If you click the Quick Add button, the vendor name will be added exactly as you've typed it, but you'll have to add the vendor's address and other data later. To enter all the vendor's information now, click the Set Up button and you'll see the New Vendor form. (If you're not sure what to do with this form, click the How Do I? button and choose one of the options from the pop-up menu.)

REMINDING YOURSELF ABOUT VENDOR DISCOUNTS

To take advantage of early-payment discounts from vendors, enter the Due Date as the date by which the early payment is due. QuickBooks will list the bill on the Reminders list and remind you to pay the bill on the early payment date so you'll get the discount. For more information about using the Reminders list, choose Lists > Reminders and then choose an option from the How Do I? pop-up menu.

Entering Bill Details

When you fill out the Bill Details section, you must first click the Items or Expenses tab to indicate the type of expense. The choice you make here determines how the bill's costs are recorded. For example, if you pay an electricity bill, you would record it as an expense:

1. Click the Expenses tab.

2. Click inside the detail area. The columns in the form will look like the ones shown in Figure 6.5.

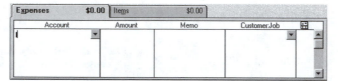

Figure 6.5 Tabs on the Enter Bills form let you record the bill's contents as items or expenses.

 ***Note:** If you're using classes to track your expenses, there will be an additional Class column in the detail area of the Enter Bills and Write Checks forms.*

3. Choose the expense account (probably Utilities or Electricity) from the pop-up list, then press Tab and enter the amount.

4. To assign the expense to a customer (for example, if you paid an electricity bill for a house under construction), choose a customer and job with the Customer:Job column's pop-up list. When you do this, the invoice icon appears to the right, indicating that the expense is billable to that customer and job. If you don't want to pass on the expense to a customer, click the icon to place an X over it.

5. If you're tracking expenses by class, choose one with the pop-up list in the Class column.

Note: *It's essential for you to be consistent in assiging expenses to different accounts and classes because that's the only way QuickBooks knows which transaction belongs where. When making an accounts payable report, for example, QuickBooks sorts your payables by expense account. If you assign an expense to the wrong account, the report will be wrong.*

Tip: *If you correct an amount in the detail area and you want to see how the change affects the total amount on the bill shown above, press Tab or click the Recalc button.*

6. Click the Items tab to enter expense information for any items on the bill.

7. Click OK or Next to record the transaction.

Receiving Inventory

When you receive inventory, you add the items to your QuickBooks inventory records, record the vendor's bill for the items, and close the purchase order you wrote for the items, if you wrote one.

Receiving Items with an Enclosed Bill

If there is a bill enclosed with the shipment, you can receive the inventory and enter the bill at the same time.

1. Choose Activities > Inventory > Receive Items and Enter Bill. You'll see the Enter Bills form shown in Figure 6.6.

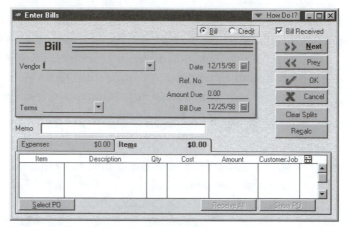

Figure 6.6 The Enter Bills form.

This form is similar to the Enter Bills form shown in Figure 6.3, but it has a Select PO button at the bottom. Notice that the Items tab is selected automatically in the detail area because QuickBooks assumes you're receiving inventory items.

2. Select the vendor's name from the pop-up list.

3. If you previously wrote a purchase order for the items you're receiving, you'll be asked if you want to receive against that purchase order (see Figure 6.7).

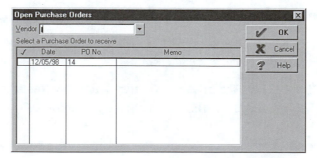

Figure 6.7 The Purchase Orders list.

4. Click in the checkmark column next to the purchase order that matches your shipment then click the OK button. The information on it (items, amounts, prices, vendor, and so on) is automatically

transferred to the detail area of the Enter Bills form. (If you don't have an outstanding purchase order for this item receipt, fill in the detail area manually.)

5. If you're tracking item purchases by class, choose a class for each received item with the Class pop-up list in the detail area.

6. To add other expenses that apply to the entire shipment, such as freight, click the Expenses tab and enter them there.

7. Click the OK, Next, or Previous button to store the information.

Receiving Items without a Bill

If you receive items without an enclosed bill, there's a different version of the same form to use.

1. Choose Activities > Inventory > Receive Items. The Create Item Receipts form shown in Figure 6.8 opens.

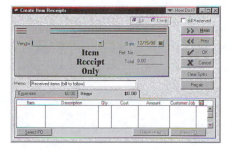

Figure 6.8 The Create Item Receipts form.

 Note: *This form is almost the same as the Enter Bills form shown in Figure 6.6. In fact, if you check the Bill Received checkbox, this form becomes the Receive Items and Enter Bills form.*

2. Type in the vendor's name or choose it from the pop-up list. If you have open purchase orders for this vendor, a message will ask if you want to receive against them.

3. Click the OK button to see a list of purchase orders from this vendor.

4. Click in the checkmark column to select the purchase order against which the items will be received then click the OK button. The Items detail area of the form will be filled in. (If you don't have a P.O. for this shipment, enter the shipment details manually in the detail area.)

5. If some items, quantities, or prices are different from your original P.O., make corrections manually in the detail area.

6. Choose a class for each received item with the Class pop-up list, if you're tracking classes.

7. Click the OK, Next, or Previous button to record the data.

Matching a Bill to Previously Received Items

When you eventually do receive a bill for items that you previously recorded as received, you should reconcile your inventory account by indicating that you now have a bill for those items.

1. Choose Activities > Inventory > Enter Bill for Rec'd Items. The Select Item Receipt form shown in Figure 6.9 appears.

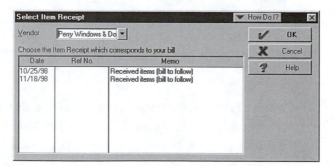

Figure 6-9 The Select Item Receipt form.

2. Choose the vendor name from the pop-up list. You'll see a list of dated item receipts.

3. Click on the receipt that matches the bill you're entering then click the OK button. QuickBooks records the bill receipt and displays the

Enter Bills form you previously used to enter the item receipt. You'll notice that the Bill Received checkbox is now checked on this Enter Bills form.

ADJUSTING INVENTORY LEVELS OR VALUES

If you do a physical inventory and you need to adjust the counts of items in stock, choose Activities > Inventory > Adjust Qty/Value on Hand. Then, select the item whose quantity you want to change in the list that appears and type in the new quantity in the appropriate column. QuickBooks automatically adjusts the value of the items on hand.

Writing Checks

We consider paying bills a weekly or monthly activity so we discuss writing checks against bills previously entered in Chapter 7, "Weekly and Monthly Activities." But sometimes you just want to write a check without having to enter a bill first. You might take some cash out of the company as an owner's draw, for example, or you might pay for an item or service at the time you buy it.

WRITING CHECKS VERSUS ENTERING BILLS

Since you can code each check with a customer and job name on the check form's detail area, you can always assign expenses for which you write checks to specific customers, just as you do when you enter a bill. But when you use the Enter Bills form, you can enter a due date and QuickBooks automatically adds that bill to your Reminders list so you'll be reminded about it. It's best to use the Enter Bills form unless you're just writing a check on the fly.

The Write Checks Form

When you write a check you fill in a check-like form, but you also fill in a detail area where you specify the goods or services you're paying for so this data can be added to the appropriate expense account. To write a check:

1. Choose Activities > Write Checks. A blank check form will appear with today's date on it (see Figure 6.10).

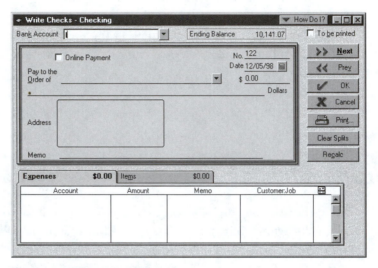

Figure 6-10 The Write Checks form.

2. Select the correct bank account from the Bank Account pop-up list, if necessary.

3. Choose the vendor name from the pop-up list or enter a new name.

4. If you'll be paying with an online payment, click the Online Payment checkbox. (See "Using Online Banking" in Chapter 7.)

5. Enter the numeric amount of the check. QuickBooks will automatically enter the written-out version of the number on the line below and it will also enter the total amount of the check in the first line of the detail area.

6. Click either the Expenses or Items tab in the detail area to choose the type of expense. (See "Entering Bill Details" earlier in this chapter for more information about this.)

7. Click in the Account column of the detail area and then choose an expense category from the pop-up list.

8. Enter the amount of the expense.

9. If you want to assign the expense to a particular customer or job, choose one from the Customer:Job pop-up list.

10. If you're tracking expenses by class, select a class from the Class pop-up list.

11. If this check is for more than one expense, list each expense in a separate row of the detail area.

12. Click OK to store the new check for printing later or click Print to print this one check immediately.

SPLITTING TRANSACTIONS

When you enter a bill you've received or write a check, you may often need to divide the total amount of the bill or check into several different specific expenses. For example, a credit card bill of $200.00 might be split among half a dozen different expenses for entertainment, fuel, supplies, and so on. To split a transaction, all you have to do is enter all of the specific expense categories and amounts that make up a bill or check in the detail area. To remove split transaction details, click the Clear Splits button at the right side of the check or bill form.

Check Printing Options

You can print each check as you fill it out by clicking the Print button or you can store a group of checks and print them as a batch. To save a check for batch printing, check the To Be Printed checkbox at the upper-right corner of the form before clicking the OK button to store the transaction. When you're ready to print the batch of checks, choose File > Print Forms > Print Checks. You'll see a list of checks in the batch so you can review them before printing.

If you're using a paper checkbook and you write checks by hand or on a typewriter, uncheck the To Be Printed checkbox on the Write Checks form so your checks won't be queued for printing.

Ordering Checks

You can order checks in a variety of formats to suit your needs. There are single-check (or voucher check) forms for laser or ink-jet printers, two- or three-up checks for laser or ink-jet printers, or continuous checks for dot-matrix printers.

You may want to use voucher checks for your payroll because they provide a stub for the employee and another stub for your records. Since you only print one check per sheet of paper, however, voucher checks are more expensive to use than three-up checks. As a result, you may want to use a set of voucher checks for payroll only and a set of three-up checks or continuous checks for other purposes. If you order two sets of checks, order one set with a starting number that is much higher than the other set's starting number (for example, 8001 compared to 201). This way, you'll quickly be able to tell which checks are for which purpose by looking at the number series.

Receiving Payments

As you receive payments from customers, you'll want to record them as soon as possible to keep your accounts receivable records up to date. The basic process for receiving payments is covered in "Entering a Customer Payment" in Chapter 4, but let's look at some details.

QuickBooks assumes you want to clear your outstanding invoices in order, from oldest to newest, so it always tries to apply payments to the oldest invoices for each customer. However, you can manually select a specific invoice when applying a payment.

1. Choose Activities > Receive Payments and then select a name from the Customer:Job pop-up list. The Receive Payments form will list any outstanding invoices for that customer as shown in Figure 6.11.

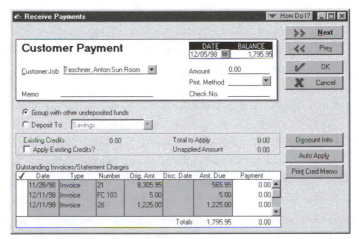

Figure 6.11 When you receive payments, QuickBooks lists outstanding invoices for the customer.

 Note: *The Receive Payments function assumes you've already sent an invoice to a customer. If you type in a new customer name on the form, you'll be asked to add the customer's information.*

2. Enter the amount of the payment you've received on the Amount line and press Tab.

    • If there's only one invoice outstanding for this customer, Quick-Books will automatically apply the amount received against that invoice.

    • If the payment matches the total of two or more invoices, Quick-Books will automatically apply the payments against the appropriate invoices, placing a checkmark in the checkmark column and showing the amount paid in the Payment column. (Once you click OK to store the data, these invoices will be removed from your accounts receivable list.)

    • If the payment doesn't match the total of one or more invoices, QuickBooks will apply it against the oldest invoice on the list.

3. If you don't want the payment automatically applied as above, un-check the invoice(s) against which the payment is applied (click in the checkmark column to remove the checkmark), then check the invoice to which you do want the payment applied. Any invoice you make a partial payment against will remain on your accounts receivable list—with the amounts due on it adjusted accordingly—until the invoice is completely paid.

Tip: *The Unapplied Amount on the Receive Payments form will be retained as a credit if you store the transaction without applying it to an invoice. You can either print a credit memo immediately or simply store the credit for future use. See "Applying Credits," next.*

4. Click the OK button to record the information.

For more information about receiving payments, check out the topics under "receiving payments" in the Help system index.

Applying Credits

If you've received an advance payment or if a customer has a credit balance with you, you can apply it to an outstanding invoice at any time.

1. Choose Activities > Receive Payments to display the Receive Payments form and choose the customer and job name from the Customer:Job pop-up list. The invoices that customer owes you will appear in the list at the bottom of the form.

2. Check the Apply Existing Credits checkbox to apply the credit against the oldest invoice(s) in the list.

Applying Discounts

You can set up a standard discount for any customer when you initially enter the customer information, but you may also want to offer discounts for specific bills. To apply a discount to a particular bill:

1. Display the Receive Payments form.

2. Select the customer:job.

3. Click in the checkmark column at the bottom of the form to select the invoice you want to discount.

4. Click the Discount Info button. You'll see the Discount Information dialog box shown in Figure 6.12.

Figure 6.12 You can apply discounts to specific invoices with the Discount Information dialog box.

5. Type the amount of the discount then choose an expense account (so you can track the discount as an expense).

6. Click the OK button to record the discount. The Receive Payments form will now reflect the discounted amount due for this invoice.

Tip: *You can always view the original amount of the invoice by selecting it on the Receive Payments form and clicking the Discount Info button.*

For more information about applying a discount to a customer's bill, check out one of the topics under "discounts" in the Help system index.

Depositing a Customer Payment

When you receive a customer payment, you can also record a deposit of this payment to your checking account register—right on the same form. To do this, click the Deposit To button on the Receive Payments form then choose the checking or savings account name where you want to record the deposit. The default choice here is Group with Other Undeposited Funds because QuickBooks assumes you'll use a separate deposit slip form to enter the deposit in your checking register at a later time.

When to Tell QuickBooks about Deposits

Whenever you indicate a deposit in QuickBooks (on the Make Deposit or Receive Payments forms), the deposit is recorded in your checking account register. But of course, the money isn't actually available to you until you take it to the bank. We think it's dangerous to add money to your QuickBooks checking account register long before you actually deposit it at the bank.

When you fill out the Receive Payments form, it's better to accept the default option—Group With Other Undeposited Funds—so the payment is simply stored for a future deposit. Then, when you fill out a deposit slip with the Make Deposit form, the undeposited funds will be automatically listed on the deposit slip. Don't prepare a deposit slip form until you're ready to go to the bank. That way, you'll be adding funds to your checkbook register at about the same time they are actually deposited at the bank.

Making Deposits

When you receive money, you can tell QuickBooks about it either by using the Receive Payments form (discussed above) or by filling out a deposit slip. Using a deposit slip has some advantages, however. You can use a deposit slip form to record income other than customer payments and you can also print the slip and use it when you go to the bank.

To create a deposit slip, you use one form to select received monies to deposit and another to review the deposit details.

1. Choose Activities > Make Deposits. You'll see the Payments to Deposit form shown in Figure 6.13.

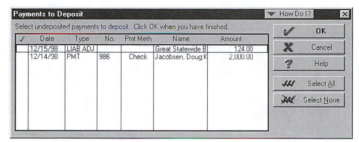

Figure 6.13 The Payments to Deposit form.

2. If you grouped customer payments with undeposited funds when you filled out the Receive Payments form, you'll see a list of undeposited payments. Click in the checkmark column in the detail area to select any payments you want to add to the current deposit slip (or click the Select All button), then press Return or click OK to display the Make Deposits form.

The Make Deposits form that appears in Figure 6.14 shows each payment you're depositing.

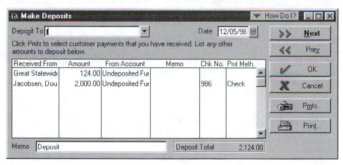

Figure 6.14 The Make Deposits form can be printed as a deposit slip for your bank.

3. Select the account to which you want to make the deposit and change the date of the deposit if it's different from the current date.

4. Enter the details about other deposits in individual lines in the detail area. (For example, you may be putting cash into the business.) The Deposit Total area at the bottom will automatically recalculate the total as you add items.

5. To print the deposit slip, click the Print button. QuickBooks will print a deposit slip that shows all the transactions you selected or entered; it will also include the name of your bank, your name and address, and your account number.

Tracking Time

You track time in QuickBooks Pro for two main reasons. You need to know how much time your employees work so you can pay them and you need to know how much time they spend on each customer's jobs so you can bill your customers for it. In order to have time information available for invoices or paychecks, you must record it with QuickBooks Pro's Time Tracking features. These features are not available in the standard version of QuickBooks.

TIME AND PAY RATES AREN'T THE SAME

When you track time, you track only the hours your employees work (either total hours, or hours spent on certain jobs for certain customers during a pay period). On the other hand, you pay each employee one or more hourly wage rates. You can set up varying pay rates by storing them in the Payroll Information section of the employee's information form. See ""payroll setup" in the Help system index.

When you bill customers for employee time, you use service items. You'll probably have a separate service item for each type of service you provide (for example, one rate for copy writing and one for art direction). To create these service items, display the Items list, choose the New command with the Item menu button, choose the Service type, and then enter the hourly rate for that service. (See "service item setup" in the Help system index for more information.)

QuickBooks has three different tools for tracking time.

*   You can record single-time activities (one group of hours at one rate for one customer) on individual forms. This is the best method if

you estimate hours spent for each client on a daily basis. You might also use the single-activity method when an employee normally works for you but occasionally does work that is charged to a customer. Data from the single-activity forms is automatically transferred to the employee's weekly timesheet.

- You can record total employee hours and details on a timesheet. Use this method for entering weekly time records for payroll and for your own internal tracking of how employees spend their time.

- If you're an architect, lawyer, or another type of consultant and you bill by the quarter hour, it's easiest to use the QuickBooks Pro Timer. You can use the QuickBooks Pro Timer to keep detailed records of every minute you spend on different tasks for different clients throughout the day and then export those records to a timesheet in QuickBooks.

Let's look at each method in turn.

Recording Single-Time Activities

Here's how to record a single-time activity:

1. Choose Activities > Time Tracking > Enter Single Activity. You'll see the Enter Single Activity form shown in Figure 6.15.

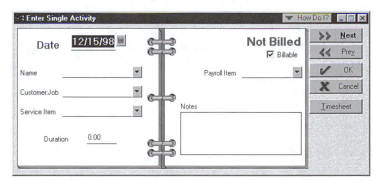

Figure 6.15 Use the Enter Single Activity form to record individual time charges.

Note: *This form says Not Billed in the upper-right corner because this time segment has not yet been billed to a customer.*

2. Choose the employee's name from the Name pop-up list.

3. Choose the customer and job, and service item from their respective pop-up lists.

4. Type a decimal number indicating the number of hours (or fraction thereof) in the Duration blank

5. Choose a Payroll Item type (such as Salary or Wages) from the pop-up menu. Payroll Item type information will be transferred to the employee's paycheck. By indicating this information here, you tell QuickBooks how to classify the hours so it can properly figure the pay rate when you do payroll. (You may have two or more pay rates for an employee.)

6. Click the OK, Next, or Previous button to record the time activity.

 Note: *Click the Next or Previous buttons to view the previous or following single-activity time form or click the Timesheet button to view a current weekly timesheet form for this employee.*

Recording Times on a Weekly Timesheet

To record times all at once, use the weekly timesheet:

1. Choose Activities > Time Tracking > Use Weekly Timesheet. You'll see a timesheet form like the one shown in Figure 6.16.

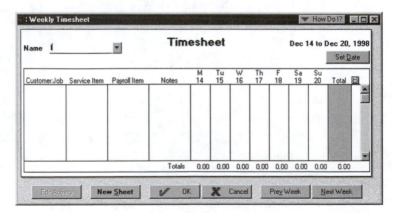

Figure 6.16 The Weekly Timesheet form.

Note: *Click the Set Date button to view or record times for a period other than the current one.*

2. Choose an employee name from the pop-up list at the upper-left corner.

3. Fill in the information about the customer and job, service item, payroll item, and hours per day in the detail area below. (You'll see pop-up lists for customer:job, payroll item, and service item when you click in the detail area.)

 Tip: *Enter data about one customer:job at a time, using one row in the detail area for each type of work. For example, if an employee did the same type of work for the same customer:job on Monday, Wednesday, and Thursday, you would select that customer:job and record all the hours for those days in that one row of the detail area. But if the employee did carpentry work on Monday (at one pay rate) and general labor on Wednesday and Thursday (at another pay rate), there would be separate rows for each type of labor for this customer.*

4. Click the OK button to store the information.

Using the QuickBooks Pro Timer

The QuickBooks Pro Timer is a separate program that comes only with QuickBooks Pro. You'll find it inside the QuickBooks Pro folder on your hard disk. The Timer allows you to record specific activities for specific employees down to the minute and then export that data so it can be read into a QuickBooks time record for billing.

 Note: *If you don't see the QuickBooks Timer program in the QuickBooks folder on your hard disk, install the Timer from the QuickBooks program CD.*

To use the Timer, you'll need to export your QuickBooks data file's list information, create a new Timer File, and import the list information into it. This way, you'll be able to choose different customers and jobs from pop-up lists inside the Timer window. Once you've imported your list information into the Timer, you'll create new timed activities and then record times for them. After you've recorded times for a billing period, you must export them to QuickBooks Pro for use in invoices or payroll activities.

Setting up a Timer File

To create a Timer file:

1. Choose File > Timer Activities > Export Lists for Timer. You'll see the wizard screen shown in Figure 6.17 that explains the process of exporting list data for use in a Timer file.

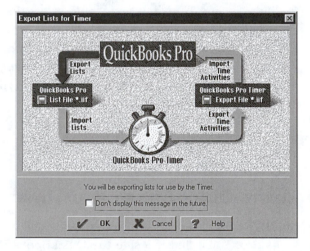

Figure 6.17
The Export Lists for Timer wizard.

2. Click the OK button. You'll see a standard File Save dialog box where you can name the new list data file.

3. Type in a name for the new file, but don't change the .iif file extension–the Timer program only recognizes that extension when importing list data.

4. Click the OK button. You'll see a message when the data is exported successfully.

5. Choose Start > Programs > QuickBooks Pro > QuickBooks Timer. You'll see the dialog box shown in Figure 6.18 asking you to name or open a Timer file.

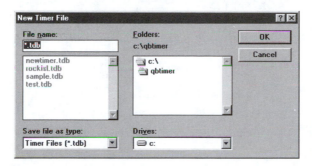

Figure 6.18
The New Timer
File dialog box.

6. Click the Create New Timer file option and then click OK. You'll see a standard File Open dialog box.

7. Select the QuickBooks data file you just exported and click the OK button to import it. You'll see a message when the list data is successfully imported and you'll see the Timer window shown in Figure 6.19.

Figure 6.19 The QuickBooks Pro Timer window.

You're now ready to create new activities and record times.

Creating a New Time Activity

The Timer window lets you track your activities to the minute and assign them to specific customers or jobs. You can store many different activities in the Timer window and then simply choose the one you want as you change tasks during the day. To create a new activity:

1. Click the New Activity button in the Timer window. You'll see the New Activity form shown in Figure 6.20.

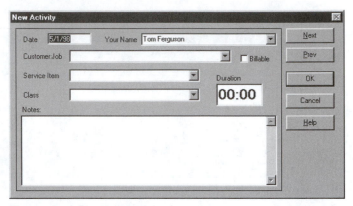

Figure 6.20 The New Activity form.

2. Choose your name from the Your Name pop-up list.

3. Select a Customer:Job, service item, and class (if you're tracking classes) from the other pop-up lists.

4. Click OK to create the activity. You'll see the new activity listed in the Timer window.

Recording a Time Activity

Once you have defined an activity, you can record time spent on it. To record a time activity:

1. Open your Timer file to display the Timer window.

2. Choose a predefined activity from the Activity pop-up list or click the New Activity button to create a new one.

3. Click the Start button. The Timer starts recording. You can tell it's recording because the colon (:) between the hours and minutes is blinking and the Start button name has changed to Stop.

4. When you're finished with the task, click the Stop button. The time duration will be recorded for this vendor and activity in the Timer data file.

Tip: *Once you create an activity, it is available on the Current Activity list. Although you can only time one activity at once, the other activities and the times recorded for them are preserved. To temporarily stop working on an activity, click the Stop button and then choose or create another current activity to time. To resume timing a previous activity, choose it from the Current Activity list and then click the Resume button to start its timer again.*

Editing a Time Activity

You can edit the customer:job, vendor, time duration, service item, or class for an activity at any time.

1. Choose the activity from the Current Activity pop-up list.

2. Click the Edit Activity button. You'll see the Edit Activity form, which looks like the New Activity form in Figure 6.20.

3. Select the data you want to change and either choose new data from pop-up lists or type it in.

4. Click the OK button to record your changes.

USING THE TIMER WITH MULTIPLE EMPLOYEES

You can use the Timer with more than one employee by distributing the Timer program to each person who needs it and asking them to track their own time individually. After all employees keep track of time during a pay or billing period, you can have each of them export a Timer data file to you (by saving it on the network server or attaching it to an email document). Once you have all the Timer files you need for a payroll or invoice, just import them one by one.

Exporting Time Activity Data

After you have recorded all your timed activities for a billing period, you need to export the Timer file.

1. Choose File > Export Time Activities from the menu inside the Timer window. You'll see a wizard screen that explains what you're about to do.

2. Click the Continue button and you'll see a File Save dialog box where you can name the Timer data file.

3. Type a name for the file, making sure not to change the extension, and click the OK button.

Tip: *Be sure to give your Timer file a distinctive name so you can easily locate the right file when you import it into QuickBooks Pro.*

Importing Time Activity Data

Once you've exported data from the QuickBooks Pro Timer, you need to import it into QuickBooks Pro.

1. Start QuickBooks Pro if it's not already running.

2. Choose File > Timer Activities > Import Activities from Timer. You'll see a wizard screen that explains what you're about to do.

3. Click the OK button and you'll see a File Open dialog box where you can import the Timer data file you created.

4. Select the file and click the Open button. The Timer data will be stored in your QuickBooks data file. Each timed activity will be transferred to a Single Time Activity form and you can see all activities for each employee on the Weekly Timesheet form.

Making Estimates

If you're using QuickBooks Pro, you can use an Estimates form to detail work or products you propose to sell to your prospective customer. Writing an estimate is very similar to writing an invoice because an estimate is essentially a guess about what the invoice will eventually contain. You can write a custom estimate for a particular customer, or you can "memorize" an estimate so you can easily recall and reuse it for other jobs.

Tip: *You can also turn an estimate into an invoice and bill for work in progress or for the entire amount. See "Invoicing for Work in Progress" in Chapter 7.*

The Create Estimates Form

To create an estimate, you use the Create Estimates form.

1. Choose Activities > Create Estimates. You'll see the Create Estimates form shown in Figure 6.21.

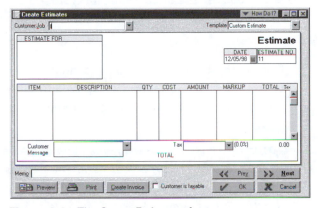

Figure 6.21 The Create Estimates form.

1. Choose a customer and job name and a class (if necessary) at the top of the form

2. Fill in the estimate number and customer address (if it isn't entered automatically when you select the customer name).

 Tip: *If you're estimating a job for an existing customer, it's easier to display the Customer:Job list (Lists > Customers:Jobs), select the customer and job name, and then choose the Create Estimate button with the Activities menu button. When you do this, QuickBooks automatically fills in the customer name and address information on the new estimate form.*

4. In the detail area below, select items from the pop-up list, and the description and cost of those items will automatically be filled in. You can also enter a markup for individual items in the detail area if you like.

QuickBooks automatically calculates item totals for you based on the item quantities you enter, and it automatically adds tax to the estimate based on a sales tax rate you entered in the initial setup interview.

Note: *The Tax blank has to be filled in whether or not the customer or estimated items are taxable because QuickBooks needs to know about nontaxable sales for your quarterly and yearly tax reports. If the work isn't taxable, enter 0%.*

5. Click in the T (taxable) column to indicate whether or not the item is taxable. This information is supplied from the item's information you initially entered when you added the item to your company file.

Tip: *In the Customer message box, you can select from a list of predefined messages or type your own. You can also view all the messages on this list (or add new ones) by choosing Lists > Other Lists > Customer Messages.*

Memorizing an Estimate

If you create an estimate and want to store it for use with other customers later, choose Edit > Memorize Estimate while the estimate is displayed. You'll be given a chance to name the estimate and it will then be stored without the customer name. You can recall a memorized estimate any time by choosing Lists > Memorized Transactions.

Finding Transactions

As you begin to fill up your QuickBooks data file with invoices, receipts, checks, purchase orders, and other transactions, you'll probably need to locate specific transactions from time to time. You can always flip through previously stored transactions one at a time by clicking the Prev button in the form window, but it's usually much faster to use the Find command.

Opening the Find Dialog Box

To open the Find dialog box:

1. Choose Edit > Find or press Ctrl+F. The Find window shown in Figure 6.22 opens.

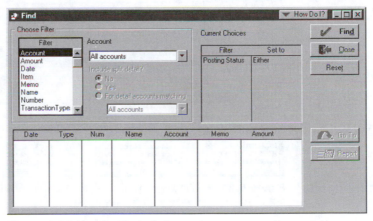

Figure 6.22 Use the Find window to locate transactions quickly.

Locating Transactions

1. In the Find dialog box, you use the Choose Filter list and the accompanying options to specify the method you want used to locate the transaction(s). As you choose filter options, you'll see them listed in the Current Choices list at the right.

2. Choose a filter option from the Filter list. Each filter has its own options to make your search even more specific. For example, if you choose Account as the filter, you'll have options to find transactions by a specific account. Scroll down the Filter list to see all the filters you can use. There are plenty of choices.

3. Specify the options for the filter you chose. The filter and option you specified will be added to the Current Choices list.

4. Choose additional filters and options, if you like.

5. Click Find when your filter is complete. QuickBooks will locate all the transactions that match your filter and will list them at the bottom of the window (see Figure 6.23).

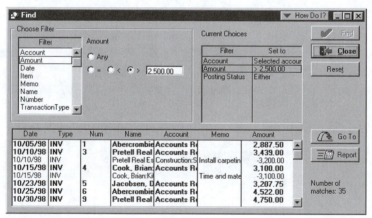

Figure 6.23 The Find window lists all the transactions it finds; double-click a transaction to display it.

Each found transaction is listed in bold. If a transaction includes line or detail items that contribute to the total amount, the line items or detail amounts are listed below it.

6. Double-click any transaction (or select it and click the Go To button at the right) to display that transaction. You'll see that transaction's form.

7. Choose Window > Find or Edit > Find or press Ctrl-F to return to the Find window and view other transactions.

8. Click the Close button to put away the Find window.

Editing a Find Filter

If you make a mistake in specifying a filter, you can correct the problem in two different ways:

*   Click the Reset button to clear all the filters from the Current Choices list and start over.

*   Click on a particular filter in the Current Choices list to select it and then press the Delete key to remove it.

7

WEEKLY AND MONTHLY ACTIVITIES

In this chapter, we'll focus on activities you perform on a regular weekly or monthly schedule. Most companies follow fixed cycles for paying bills, preparing invoices and purchase orders, handling payroll, and reconciling checking accounts. Regular cycles make it easier to capture the data necessary to perform these activities. For example, sending out invoices just after each payroll cycle allows you to collect all the time expenses you incurred on the customer's behalf before you prepare the invoices. Paying bills once a month allows you time to receive the goods or services you're paying for and it helps make your cash flow more predictable. Sending out purchase orders once a week allows you to focus on this one activity only at that time.

Let's look at these regularly scheduled activities one at a time.

Creating Invoices

You may choose to create invoices weekly or monthly, but in either case, you'll need to have available all the data that supports each invoice total. You'll need the following:

- The customer's name and address.

- Your work orders or estimates.

- Customer purchase orders.

- Sales receipts for items you bought on the customer's behalf.

- Time or payroll records (to bill for hours spent on each customer's job).

- The markup rate you want to apply to labor or materials.

Most of this information will already be stored in QuickBooks if you're invoicing an existing customer and you've captured the appropriate time and expense data before preparing the invoice.

You use the Create Invoices form to make any invoice and you can also use it to review invoices you previously made. To make an invoice:

1. Choose Activities > Create Invoices then choose a name from the Customer:Job pop-up list at the top-left of the form. The form will look like Figure 7.1.

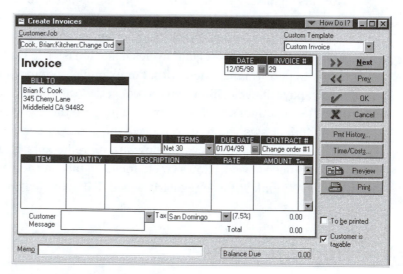

Figure 7.1 The Create Invoices form.

Tip: *You can display different invoice formats by choosing a differ-ent template from the Custom Template pop-up list at the top of the Create Invoices form. See "Customizing Form Templates" in Chapter 5 for more information on creating and using templates.*

Note: *If you previously created an estimate for the customer you choose to invoice, you'll be given a chance to create an invoice from that estimate. See "Invoicing for Work in Progress," later in this chapter.*

2. Choose the job's class (if any) from the Class pop-up list.

3. Enter different dates or invoice numbers if you don't like the ones QuickBooks suggests. Since you selected an existing customer:job name, the Bill To box already contains the customer's full name and address information, along with data about this customer's terms and tax rate.

4. Enter a purchase order number, if you like.

   In this example, we've been tracking the time and material costs for this customer, so you can now see exactly what this customer currently owes you.

5. Click the Time/Costs button at the right of the form. You'll see the Choose Billable Time & Costs dialog box, which lists all of the time and items charged to this job that haven't yet been billed. (See Figure 7.2.).

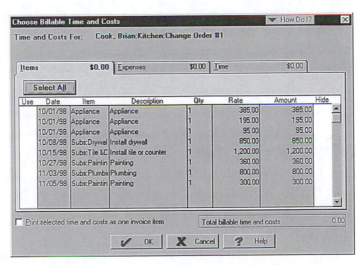

Figure 7.2 The Choose Billable Time & Costs form for the same invoice.

Notice there are tabs for different groups of charges: Items, Expenses, and Time.

6.   Click the appropriate tab at the top of the detail area to see a list of expenses in one of the three categories.

7.   Click in the Use column next to the individual item(s) you want to add to the invoice, or click the Select All button to choose them all.

 Tip: *You can choose to show all selected time and cost items as one item on an invoice by checking the Print Selected Time and Costs as One Invoice Item checkbox at the lower-left corner of the Choose Billable Time and Costs dialog box.*

8.   Repeat this process for the other types of charges by clicking their tabs.

As you add items to the invoice, the total of the items you've selected appears in the lower-right corner of the form.

9.   Click the OK button when you're done to return to the Create Invoices form.

 Tip: *You can edit the items listed on the Create Invoices form at any time. If you want to use a more specific description of a particular item, for example, just select the item's description in the invoice detail area and type a different one.*

10.   Click in the next empty row of the detail area and then add any discount, markup, or subtotal items, if you want to include these. To add a subtotal, for example, click in the Item column in an empty row and choose the subtotal item from the pop-up list. See the example in Figure 7.3.

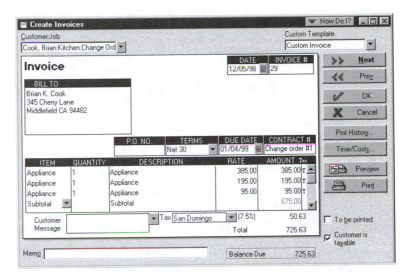

Figure 7.3 The same invoice with appliance costs and a subtotal item added.

Note: *If there are no subtotal or markup items on your Item list, add them. See "Completing the Item List" in Chapter 4 for more information.*

Now this invoice contains includes a subtotal for the appliances.

Note: *QuickBooks adds items to the invoice detail area in order and you can't change the order once you've added them. If you want to add a subtotal for a group of items on an invoice, add the items in the group one after the other, and then add the subtotal immediately afterward before adding new items not included in the subtotal.*

Sales tax is added automatically because we have previously indicated that the customer is taxable. If for some reason you wish to change that tax status, unchecking the Customer is Taxable box in the lower-right corner of the invoice form will remove the tax charge.

11. Click the OK, Next, or Prev button to store the invoice data.

SUBTOTALS, MARKUPS, AND OTHER ITEMS

You typically think of items on an invoice as goods or services, but there are other items you may want to add. On your Items list, you'll find a Subtotal item, and you can add others. When you add the Subtotal item to an invoice, it produces a subtotal of all the items listed above it, up to the previous subtotal.

You can create other items for various discounts or markups as well. For example, you might have an item called Markup that takes 20 percent of the subtotal and adds it to the invoice total. Contractors frequently add a markup for their supervision labor. To create an item that marks up an invoice subtotal, create a new item of the Other Charges type then type in the percentage markup you want applied. The same is true for discounts—if you're having a sale or selling a certain volume of product to a customer, you can use a discount item to apply the discount to an invoice. See "other charge items" in the Help system index for more information.

Invoicing for Work in Progress

If you're in a service business where jobs take months to complete, you may want to send interim invoices for portions of those jobs that have been finished. There are three ways to do this:

- If you previously created an estimate for the job, QuickBooks will ask you if you want to use it when you select that job on the Create Invoices form.

- You can display the estimate form and turn it into a progress invoice. (See "Making Estimates" in Chapter 6 for more on creating estimates.)

- If you don't have a job estimate form, you can create a progress invoice by using an invoice template that includes an extra column for the percent of completion.

Creating a Progress Invoice from an Estimate

To turn an estimate into a progress invoice, you can start by displaying the estimate form.

1. Locate the estimate you want using one of these methods:

    *   Choose Activities > Create Invoices and then choose the customer and job that you previously estimated using the Customer:Job pop-up list. You'll be asked if you want to use the existing estimate for that customer. Click the OK button. You'll see the Create Progress Invoice dialog box shown in Figure 7.4. Skip to Step 3.

    *   Choose Edit > Find and locate the estimate you want to use. (See "Finding Transactions" in Chapter 6.)

    *   Choose Activities > Create Estimates to display the Create Estimates form then click the Prev button until you locate the estimate you want.

2. Click the Create Invoice button at the bottom of the estimate form. You'll see the Create Progress Invoice Based On Estimate dialog box shown in Figure 7.4.

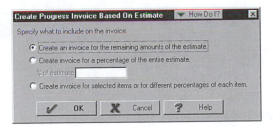

Figure 7.4 Use this dialog box to specify how charges on a progress invoice will be calculated.

3. Click one of the three radio buttons to choose how percentages of completion are applied to items on the estimate.

Invoicing by a Total Percent of Completion or by Unbilled Items

The top two options in the Create Progress Invoice Based On Estimate dialog box tell QuickBooks to automatically invoice for all previously unbilled items (remaining amounts) on the estimate, or to bill for a percentage of completion of the entire estimate. A percentage of completion for the entire invoice works best for jobs that are services, such as consulting work.

1. Click one of the top two radio buttons in the Create Progress Invoice Based On Estimate dialog box.

2. If you chose to invoice for a percentage of the entire estimate, enter a percentage in the % of Estimate box.

3. Click the OK button. You'll see a progress invoice like the one shown in Figure 7.5.

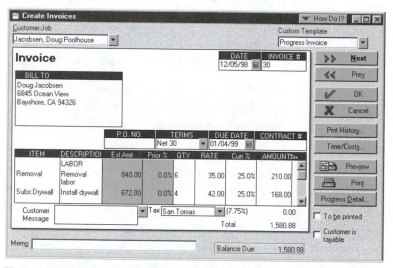

Figure 7.5 A progress invoice.

This invoice includes all the items and costs from the original estimate. Because this is a progress invoice, however, the detail area has extra columns showing the estimated amount, any previously billed completion percentages for this customer and job, and the current completion percentages for which you're invoicing today. (When you create an invoice from an estimate, QuickBooks automatically searches your invoice records and determines which items and percentages were previously billed. Pretty cool, eh?)

4. If the invoice contains service or merchandise items specified as one amount in the Rate column (rather than an hourly labor charge,

for example), enter a different amount in the Rate column to adjust it. This is necessary when a subcontractor or item ends up costing you more than you originally estimated. (You may also want to handle this by adding a new invoice item called "Price Change" or "Rate Change," however.)

5. Enter a completion percentage in the Curr % column and Quick-Books automatically calculates the amount for that item.

6. Specify percentages for remaining items on the invoice and click the OK, Next, or Prev button when you're done to store the invoice.

Invoicing Completion Percentages by Item

If you want to specify completion percentages by item, you'll need to select each item on the estimate and specify a percentage for it.

1. Click the bottom radio button in the Create Progress Invoice Based On Estimate dialog box shown in Figure 7.4 then click the OK button. You'll see the Specify Invoice Amounts for Items on Estimate dialog box where you can indicate percentages for each item as shown in Figure 7.6.

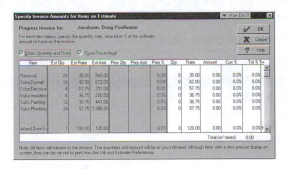

Figure 7.6 You can specify completion percentages and invoice amounts one item at a time using this dialog box.

Again, QuickBooks has searched your prior invoices and has listed the previously billed percentages and amounts in the Prior Amt and Prior % columns. In this case, there was no prior billing.

Note: *The Show Percentage checkbox must be checked in order to show the Prior % and Curr % columns in this dialog box.*

2. Select the numbers in the Curr % column and type in the percentage of completion you want to specify for each item.

3. Press the Tab key to move to the next line or click in another row of the list. QuickBooks automatically calculates the amount that will be applied to the new invoice as well as the total percentage billed.

4. Click the OK button when you're done. The progress invoice will be displayed as shown in Figure 7.5.

Making a Progress Invoice from Scratch

If you don't have an estimate for a job and you want to bill for progress on it, you can display a new invoice form and simply use the Progress Invoice template.

1. Choose Activities > Create Invoices.

2. Choose Progress Invoice from the Templates pop-up list at the top of the Create Invoices form. The progress invoice template shown in Figure 7.7 will be displayed.

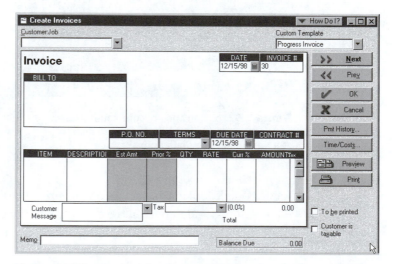

Figure 7.7 The progress invoice template.

In this case, both the Est Amt and Prior % columns are grayed out because there's no estimate from which to have taken them. (If you had previously created a progress invoice for this customer and job, the Prior % column would show previously billed percentages.)

3. Fill in the invoice as you normally would and specify a percent of completion in the Curr % column.

4. Click OK to store the invoice.

Printing Invoices, Statements, and Labels

When you've finished creating an invoice or a series of invoices, you'll naturally want to mail them out.

Printing One Invoice

To print one invoice:

1. Choose Edit > Find and locate the invoice you want to print, if it isn't on the screen already. (See "Finding Transactions" in Chapter 6.)

2. Click the Print button on the Create Invoices form. You'll see the Print One Invoice dialog box shown in Figure 7.8.

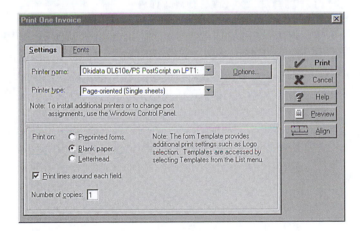

Figure 7.8 The Print One Invoice dialog box.

3. Click the Settings or Fonts tab to select options for printing, then click the Print button to print the invoice.

Printing a Group of Invoices

To print invoices in a batch:

1. Click the To be printed checkbox on each invoice you want to save for printing. The invoice is added to a batch of invoices.

2. Choose the File > Print Forms > Print Invoices. You'll see the Select Invoices to Print dialog box, where you can choose which invoices to print. All the invoices queued for printing are automatically selected.

3. Uncheck an invoice's checkmark if you don't want to print it.

4. Click the OK button. You'll see the Print Invoices dialog box, which is basically the same as the one shown in Figure 7.8. (For more information about the Select Invoices to Print dialog box, click the Help button in it.)

5. Choose printing options in the Print Invoices dialog box and then click the Print button to print the invoices.

Printing Statements

When customers owe you for more than one invoice, you can print a statement that shows a series of invoices.

1. Choose Activities > Create Statements. You'll see a dialog box like the one shown in Figure 7.9.

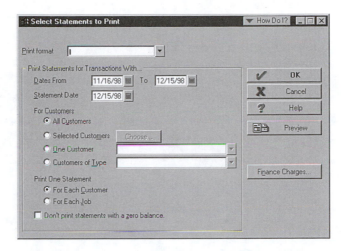

Figure 7.9
The Select
Statements
to Print
dialog box.

2. Choose the statement format you want to use from the pop-up list at the top. If you previously created one or more custom statements, they'll be on this list. If not, you can choose the Customize option on the list and customize the form now. (See "Customizing Form Templates" in Chapter 5.)

3. Enter the From and To dates (the period of activity covered by the statement) and the Statement date (the date on which you mail the statement).

4. Click the radio buttons and use the pop-up lists to choose the customers or job types for which you want to print a statement. Notice that you can choose all customers, just one customer, or all customers in a particular job type. (To choose a group of customers any other way, click the Choose button to see a list of customers and jobs, then click next to the ones you want and click the OK button.)

5. To add finance charges to one or more statements, click the Finance Charges button. You'll see the Assess Finance Charges dialog box shown in Figure 7.10.

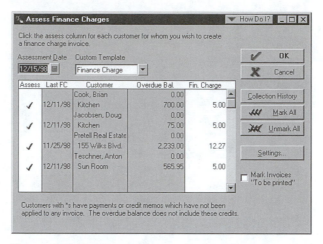

Figure 7.10 The Assess Finance Charges dialog box.

6. Click in the Assess column to add or remove finance charges for each customer or job and then click the OK button.

7. Choose an option to print statements for each customer or for each job. Notice you can also click the Don't Print Statements with a Zero Balance checkbox so you won't waste paper.

8. Click the Preview button to preview your statements or click OK or press Enter to display the Print Statements dialog box.

9. Choose the appropriate options in the Print Statements dialog box, then click Print to print the statements.

Printing Mailing Labels

If you're not using window envelopes to mail out your invoices, statements, checks, or credit memos, you can print mailing labels.

1. Choose File > Print Forms > Print Mailing Labels. You'll see the dialog box shown in Figure 7.11 where you can select the labels by customer or vendor name.

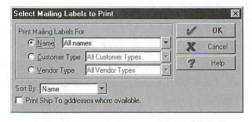

Figure 7.11 The Select Mailing Labels to Print dialog box.

2. Click a radio button to indicate the selection method then use the pop-up list, if necessary, to select a particular name, customer, or vendor.

3. Choose the sort option from the Sort By pop-up list.

4. Check the checkbox at the bottom if you want to print Ship To addresses on the labels.

5. Click the OK button or press Enter. You'll see the Print Labels dialog box shown in Figure 7.12.

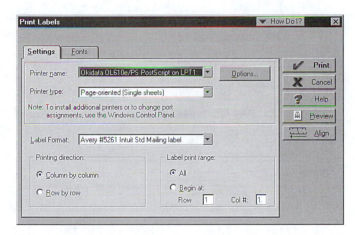

Figure 7.12 The Print Labels dialog box.

6. Choose the printer, printer feed type, label format, and other options in this dialog box.

7. Load label paper into your printer and make sure the printer is turned on.

8. Click the Print button.

Creating Purchase Orders

A purchase order is a nice way to delay spending money on the items you buy. Once you send the purchase order, vendors usually ship the item, and then it is several days or weeks before you receive the bill. In QuickBooks, a purchase order is a record of money you commit to spend; it can later be matched up against a bill for the item or service you're buying when you receive that bill.

The Create Purchase Orders Form

To make a purchase order:

1. Choose Activities > Create Purchase Orders. You'll see a form like the one shown in Figure 7.13.

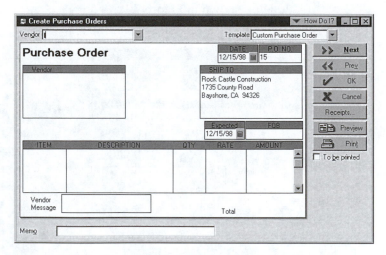

Figure 7.13 The Create Purchase Orders form.

2. Choose a vendor name from the pop-up list at the top. That vendor's name and Ship To address appear in the blanks below.

Note: *If you're creating a purchase order for a new vendor, type the vendor's full name and then press Tab. QuickBooks will tell you it can't find the vendor's record and will ask you if you want to add the information to your records now. (See "The Enter Bills form" in Chapter 6 for a description of this procedure.)*

3. If you're tracking purchases by class, choose a class with the Class pop-up list.

4. Enter the date when you expect to receive the item and add a ship-from location in the FOB (freight on board) blank, if necessary.

5. In the detail area below, click in the Item column. If you're buying items that are already recorded in your Items list, you can select the names from a pop-up list that appears in this column and the description and rate information will automatically be filled in.

6. If the item is not on your Items list, enter the item name, description, and rate (unit cost) information.

7. Enter the quantity of items. The Amount column will also be filled in, based on the quantity and rate you specified.

8. Repeat this process for additional items included on this purchase order.

9. When you're done entering items to purchase, the total amount of the purchase order appears at the bottom.

10. Type a message in the Vendor Message box to add a special note (shipping instructions, for example) and fill in the Memo blank to make a note to yourself about this purchase order.

11. Click the Print button or click the "To be printed" checkbox to print the form later.

CLEARING PURCHASE ORDERS

You can't clear a purchase order until you receive all the items or services it specified and you've logged those receipts with the Receive Items command (see "Receiving Inventory" in Chapter 6). Once you log your receipt of items for which you wrote a purchase order, display the purchase order and click the Receipts button. The items you received that were paid for through that purchase order will automatically be shown as received.

Preparing a Payroll

If you have been doing your own payroll manually, you'll be amazed at how much easier it is with QuickBooks. If you're using QuickBooks Pro and you have hourly employees, the time-tracking feature makes your payroll duties almost automatic, but QuickBooks makes payroll a breeze any way you look at it.

SAVING PAYROLL COSTS AND HASSLES

If you're having your payroll prepared by a bookkeeper or an outside service, you can save a lot of money doing it with QuickBooks, and it's a snap once you have all the pertinent employee information entered. One QuickBooks Pro user found that he could do a biweekly payroll of 13 employees in about seven minutes, including printing the paychecks.

Intuit now offers its own online payroll service that manages your payroll and guarantees accuracy. You can also arrange to have employee paychecks directly deposited to their accounts. To use these services, you must sign up, pay a monthly fee, and transmit your employee pay information to Intuit for each pay period. For more information, choose Online > Payroll Service > About the Payroll Service.

Note: *The Online Payroll and Direct Deposit services are available on a limited basis in 1998.*

Importing Employee Time Data

If you're using the QuickBooks Pro Timer, you'll need to import the Timer data files for each employee who has them. See "Importing Time Activity Data" in Chapter 6 for more information.

Selecting Employees to Pay

To pay employees, you first select which employees you want to pay. We'll assume you want to pay all of your employees in each payroll cycle.

1. Choose Activities > Payroll > Pay Employees. You'll see the Select Employees To Pay form shown in Figure 7.14.

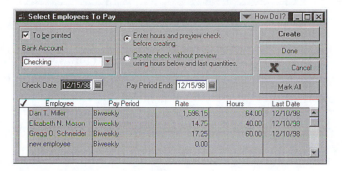

Figure 7.14 The Select Employees To Pay form.

2. Click the Mark All button to select all your employees.

3. We'll assume you want to preview each paycheck and possibly modify it, so leave the default radio button selected for this. (To simply print paychecks with the last available information—as shown in the list at the bottom of the form—click the other radio button.)

4. Click the Create button to preview the first employee's paycheck.

Previewing Paychecks

You use the Preview Paycheck dialog box shown in Figure 7.15 to review or change the information that will appear on each employee paycheck.

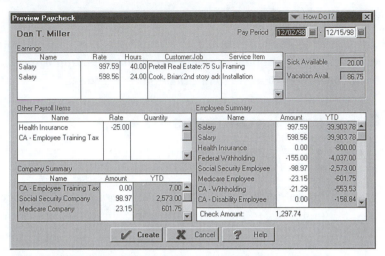

Figure 7.15 The Preview Paycheck dialog box.

If you've already been tracking this employee's time on a timesheet or single-activity time forms, or if the employee is salaried, the hour and wage information is already filled in here.

Creating a Paycheck from Scratch

If you're not using time tracking and the employee isn't salaried, the paycheck will be mostly blank and you'll have to fill in all the information manually.

1. Choose Activities > Payroll > Pay Employees and select an employee to pay.

2. Click the Create button to preview the employee's check.

3. Click in the Name column in the Earnings area and choose Wages (or Salary, or another type of pay) from the pop-up list.

4. Enter the hourly rate and the number of hours for each customer or job, or the employee's salary, in the Rate column. Fill out a separate line in the Earnings detail area for each different rate, customer, or job.

    The Employee Summary and Company Summary areas will be filled in automatically based on the earnings data you entered. This data is calculated from the payroll information you entered about the employee during the setup process. (If the check is for a new employee or the payroll information has changed, you can change the Employee summary data right on the check, or you can change the employee's payroll information. See "employee payroll records" under "payroll setup" in the Help system index.)

5. If your company makes other contributions or you have deductions for supplies, uniforms, or other items, enter them in the Other Payroll Items area.

6. When you're done with the check for this employee, click the Create button. You'll then be able to create a paycheck for the next employee on your payroll list.

Printing Paychecks

To print paychecks:

1. Choose File > Print Forms > Paychecks. The dialog box shown in Figure 7.16. will appear.

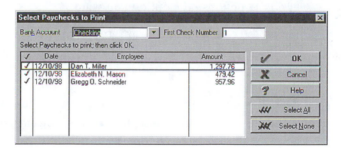

Figure 7.16 The Select Paychecks to Print dialog box.

2. Select the bank account from which the payroll checks will be paid.

3. Enter the first printed check number in the First Check Number box.

4. Click in the checkmark column next to the employees for whom you want to print paychecks, or click the Select All button to choose all of them.

5. Click the OK button. You'll see the Print Checks dialog box shown in Figure 7.17.

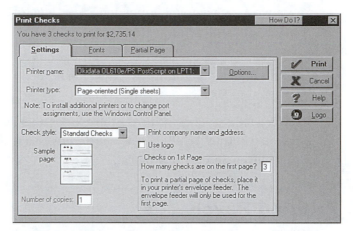

Figure 7.17 The Print Checks dialog box.

6. Choose the printer type, check style, and other options. To print a single check or a partial page of checks, click the Partial Page tab and then choose the option you want.

7. Load the checks into your printer and turn on the printer.

8. Click the Print button. QuickBooks will print your paychecks.

 Tip: _If you use voucher style checks (one per page) QuickBooks will print the withholding statement on a stub that your employees can keep for their own payroll records._

Changing Your Payroll

If you set up QuickBooks using the EasyStep Interview, you were given the opportunity to enter your employee names and basic payroll information at that time. But things change: you might give someone a raise, add or delete employees, or change a payroll expense item, for example.

If you change an employee's wage rate or other payroll information, you can record the change right on the employee's paycheck. QuickBooks will ask you if you want to make the change permanent in the employee's records, and if you do, simply click Yes.

CORRECTING INFORMATION AFTER YOU ISSUE A CHECK

If you issue a paycheck and then later have to correct it, you can cancel the original check and issue a new one, or you can make the additions or deductions on the employee's check in the following pay period. To make additions or deductions, enter them in the Other Payroll Items area of the paycheck form. For more information, see "changing" under "paychecks" in the Help system index.

However, it's easier and more straightforward to make changes on the employee's payroll information record, and you can use the same process to add or delete employees as well. All these activities are performed with the Employees list.

Changing Employee Payroll Information

To change a payroll information record:

1. Choose Lists > Employees to display the Employees list window.

2. Select the employee's name on the list and click the Edit button.

3. Click the Payroll Info tab. You can then enter the new salary or hourly wage rate.

To add a new employee:

1. Choose Lists > Employees.

2. Click the New button.

3. Fill in the information for the employee name, address, and payroll data.

 Note: *You can't delete an employee as long as the person's name is used in any transactions. You can, however, make the employee inactive on the Employee list so that person's name no longer appears there or in any pop-up lists on forms. Just choose Lists > Employees, select the employee's name in the list window, and choose Make Inactive with the Employee menu button.*

Adding or Changing Payroll Items

Payroll items such as Salary, Regular Pay, and Medicare are kept in a list, just like other groups of items in QuickBooks. To add a new payroll item:

1. Choose Lists > Payroll Items to display the Payroll Item List window.

2. Choose New with the Payroll Item menu button. You'll see the first screen of the Payroll Item wizard, where you can select the type of item you wish to create.

3. Select the item type you want and click the Next button.

4. Answer the questions on the screens that follow and click the Finish button when you're done. The new item will appear on your Payroll Items list.

To edit the information about a payroll item:

1. Choose Lists > Payroll Items to display the Payroll Item List window.

2. Double-click the item you want to edit. You'll see the Payroll Item wizard with the item's name already filled in.

3. Click the Next button and edit the information you want to change on the screens that follow, then click the Finish button when you're done.

For more information about changing payroll information, see "wages" in the Help system index.

Paying Monthly Bills

Once a month, you will have bills to pay for utilities, maintenance, postage, office supplies, credit card statements, and (less frequently) things like taxes and insurance. If you have entered these bills as they come in, paying them is a snap.

When you pay bills, you choose which bills to pay (by date or vendor), when to pay them, and how to pay them. You also have a chance to apply vendor discounts to bills if you pay them early enough. Let's take a closer look.

Selecting Bills to Pay

To view and select outstanding bills:

1. Choose Activities > Pay Bills. You'll see all the bills due as of this date, listed in Figure 7.18.

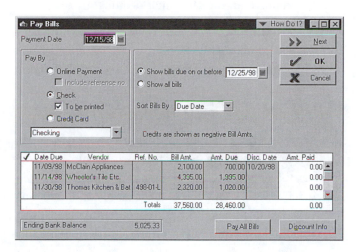

Figure 7.18 The Pay Bills form.

The detail area at the bottom lists each bill you owe along with the bill's amount, due date, early payment discount date (if any), and any amounts you may have previously paid against a bill. You can scroll the list to see other bills that are out of view.

2. If you'll be making the payments on a day other than today, enter a new payment date in the Payment Date box at the top. This is the date that will appear on checks or credit card transactions, and it's also the date on which online payments are delivered.

3. Click one of the right-hand radio button options to choose which outstanding bills to display. QuickBooks normally shows all bills due on or before the current date, but you can change the date or show all outstanding bills, if you like.

4. Choose a sorting option from the Sort Bills By pop-up list. You can sort the bills in the list below by vendor, discount date, due date, or amount due.

5. Choose a payment method with the Pay By buttons.

6. Choose which bills to pay, either by clicking in the checkmark column next to the ones you want to pay, or by clicking the Pay All Bills button at the bottom. If you make a mistake and want to re-select the bills, click the Clear Payments button at the bottom to remove all the checkmarks and start over.

7. Finally, click OK to store the bill payments. The payments will be saved as checks to be printed, credit card charges, or online payments to send, depending on which option you chose in Step 5.

APPLYING VENDOR DISCOUNTS

The Disc. Date column in the detail area of the Pay Bills form shows the last date each bill would be eligible for a discount under your payment terms with the vendor. If you're paying a bill before the discount date and you want to apply the discount, select the bill in the detail area and click the Discount Info button. You'll see the Discount Information window, where QuickBooks will have automatically calculated any discount to the bill you have selected, based on the terms you entered when you recorded the bill.

 Tip: *You can enter standard discount terms for a vendor in the Additional Information area of the New Vendor form. See "adding" under "vendors" in the Help system index.*

To apply a discount, choose a discount account (to categorize the income you get from discounts) then click the OK button. You'll be returned to the Pay Bills form and you'll see that the discount has been subtracted from the bill's total due.

About Payment Options

QuickBooks allows you to pay bills by printed or handwritten check, by charging the bill to a credit card, or with an online payment. Let's look at the check and credit card options first. For information about online payments and other online banking features, see "Using Online Banking" on the next page.

Paying by Check

If you selected the Check option in the Pay By area of the Pay Bills form, you'll need to create the check. If you checked the To Be Printed checkbox, the check will be stored for printing. To print it, choose File > Print Forms > Print Checks. (See "Check Printing Options" in Chapter 6 for more on this.)

If you didn't select the To Be Printed checkbox (so you can write checks by hand), QuickBooks automatically assigns a check number to the check and records it in the register. You can change the check number in the checking account register, if you like.

Paying with a Credit Card

When you select the Credit Card radio button and then click OK to store the transaction, QuickBooks adds the bill to your register of credit card transactions. This ensures that QuickBooks tracks the payment, but you still have to make the payment itself.

If you have set up the bill to be paid automatically each month from your credit card account, you need only enter the vendor, amount, details, and payment date on the Pay Bills form. However, if the payment isn't automatic, you'll have to remember to request that the vendor charge the bill to your credit card.

Using Online Banking

Intuit was a trailblazer in PC-based online banking with the first version of Quicken back in the 1980s, and today QuickBooks links to the Internet to make your bill payments and other banking chores much easier. With online banking, you can use QuickBooks to send electronic payments to vendors, receive up-to-the-minute bank statements, or automatically reconcile your online payment account. You can have more than one online bank account, too.

To use online banking, you'll need:

- A modem connected to your computer and a telephone line to plug the modem into.

- A bank account with a financial institution that supports electronic payments from QuickBooks.

- An online payment account with the same financial institution.

- A password or PIN (personal identification number) to access the online account from QuickBooks.

You must also set up QuickBooks to use your online connection. You can do this by choosing Online > Online Banking > Getting Started. You'll see the Getting Started with Online Banking dialog box shown in Figure 7.19. Click the Set Up Internet Access button and follow the instructions to set up QuickBooks for online access.

Applying for an Online Account

To pay bills online, you must have previously opened an account and set up online bill payments with a bank that supports online payments from QuickBooks. To see a list of institutions, choose Online > Online Banking > Financial Institutions. You'll be connected to Intuit's online list of participating banks.

If you don't have an account with a bank that supports QuickBooks online payments, you can apply for online banking at the same time you open the account with one of the participating banks. Soon after you open the account, you'll receive a confirmation letter with the password or PIN that gives you access to the account.

If you already have an account with a participating bank, you can use QuickBooks to apply for an online account with that bank:

1. Choose Online > Online Banking > Getting Started with Online Banking. You'll see the Getting Started window shown in Figure 7.19.

Figure 7.19 Getting started with online banking.

Notice you can also use this window to get general information about online banking, find a financial institution, or enable your online account once you've received a confirmation and PIN from your bank.

2. Click the Application Information button. You'll see the Online Banking Setup Interview shown in Figure 7.20.

Figure 7.20 The Online Banking Setup Interview dialog box.

3. Click the Next button and follow the instructions to complete the setup interview. When you're finished, you must then wait for a confirmation letter from your bank because this will contain the password or PIN you'll need to activate the account.

IS ONLINE BANKING SAFE?

You may be a little jittery about sending and receiving sensitive financial information through your modem, but you shouldn't be. When QuickBooks exchanges information with your online bank account, the transmission goes only from your PC to the bank's computer and it's encrypted so that it can't be read even if it is intercepted by someone else.

Dial-up transmissions like this are also used to link bank branches, ATMs, and other arms of financial institutions. These connections handle billions of transactions every day and the system has worked without incident for years. In reality, your online payments and account statements are far safer traveling over a phone line than they are traveling through postal mail.

Confirming your Online Account

Once you receive the confirmation information from your bank, you're ready to confirm the account.

1. Choose Online > Online Banking > Getting Started.

2. Click the Enable Accounts button. You'll see the Online Banking Setup wizard.

3. Click the Next button then select your online bank from the pop-up list.

4. Click the Next button, then follow the instructions to specify an account name, enter your PIN, and provide other information as QuickBooks asks you for it.

Creating Online Payments

Once your online account is set up and enabled, you're ready to pay bills electronically.

1. Choose Activities > Pay Bills to display the Pay Bills form.

2. Click the Online button in the Pay By area and select the bills you want to pay this way from the list below. If you like, you can select the bills individually and enter a different Payment Delivery date for each one in the box at the top of the form. The Payment Delivery date is the date your bank will transfer the money to the payee.

Tip: To include an invoice or credit reference number with a payment for a particular bill, select that bill, check the Include Reference No. checkbox below the Online button, and click the OK button to store this transaction by itself. Then, select all the other bills and set them up for payment without reference numbers. If you include a reference number with an online payment, your bank must print a physical check and mail it to the payee. A bank-printed check takes up to four days to be delivered.

3. Click the OK button. The bills you selected will be stored as online transactions to send.

Sending Online Transactions

When you're ready to send online transactions, you use the Online Banking Center.

1. Choose Online > Online Banking > Online Banking Center. You'll see the Online Banking Center window shown in Figure 7.21.

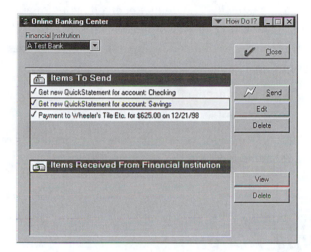

Figure 7.21 The Online Banking Center window.

2. Choose a financial institution from the pop-up list in the upper-left corner, if necessary.

   The online transactions you're about to conduct with this institution will be listed in the Items To Send list. Each item has a checkmark next to it, indicating that it will be sent during your next connection.

3. Uncheck any items you don't want to send from the Items To Send list.

4. Click the Send button. You'll be asked to enter your PIN or password.

5. Enter the PIN or password you got from your online bank and click the OK button.

6. Make sure your modem is connected and turned on. (If it's an internal modem, the dialing software will turn it on automatically.)

7. Click the OK button to connect with your bank. You'll see a message indicating that you're being connected and that you're sending or receiving transactions.

Reading Online Statements and Messages

When all items have been transmitted and received, your modem will disconnect automatically. The Items Received From Financial Institution list at the bottom of the Online Banking Center window will display the statements that were downloaded from your online accounts and any messages from your financial institution.

- To read an account register or bank message, select it in the Items Received list and click the View button.

- To delete a received item after you've read it or reconciled it, select the item and click the Delete button.

Reconciling Accounts

If you're not banking online, QuickBooks takes your word for it when it comes to balances in your checking and savings accounts, so it's important to be accurate. If you're banking online, QuickBooks can download an up-to-date bank statement and compare it with your QuickBooks account register. Either way, it's easy to reconcile your account registers with bank statements.

Reconciling from a Printed Statement

To reconcile an account from a printed statement:

1. Choose Activities > Reconcile. The Reconcile form shown in Figure 7.22 will appear.

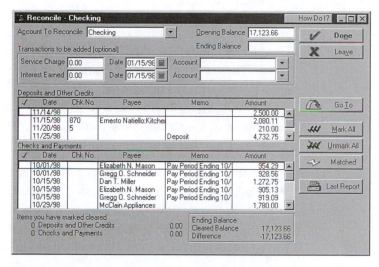

Figure 7.22 The form you use to reconcile bank accounts.

2. Select the bank account you want to reconcile from the pop-up list in the upper-left corner.

Tip: *You may want to have your account's register open when you reconcile it. In this case, choose Lists > Chart of Accounts, double-click on the account to display its register, and then choose Activities > Reconcile. The correct account will already be selected.*

The Opening Balance blank will show the closing balance from the previous month's statement (or the balance you entered as of your start date).

3. Enter the ending balance from your current statement in the Ending Balance box.

4. Enter any service charges or interest earned and the date they occurred, and assign them to the appropriate expense and income accounts using the Account pop-up lists.

5. Compare your printed statement with the Reconcile form and click in the form's checkmark column next to each deposit, check, and other charge that appears on the printed statement.

The information below the list of transactions on the Reconcile form helps you track your progress toward balancing. On the left, you can see the number of deposits and checks you've marked for reconciliation. These total numbers also appear on most bank statements, so you can tell whether or not you've missed a transaction. On the right, you can see the difference between the Cleared balance (the balance according to the transactions you've cleared in the checkmark column) and the Ending balance shown at the top of the form.

6. When there's no difference (or an insignificant difference) between the Ending Balance and the Cleared Balance at the bottom of the Reconcile form, click the Done button. QuickBooks will either tell you that your account is balanced or ask you if you want it to make an adjustment to agree with the bank statement.

7. Click the OK button. Any adjustment will be entered as such in your account's register. If you later find the reason for the adjustment (a missing check or other charge, perhaps), you can correct it by adding the charge or check to your register and deleting the adjustment entry.

8. Click the Done button to close the Reconcile form.

What about Missing Transactions?

If you find checks on your bank statement that are missing from the Reconcile form, it means you forgot to enter them in your check register. (This can happen if you use a paper checkbook for some transactions, for example, or if you have funds automatically deducted from your account.) You must clear all the checks on your bank's statement in order to balance your records. To add missing checks to the Reconcile form, double-click on the account in the Chart of Accounts list and then enter the missing checks in that account's register. The new checks you add will immediately be added to the Reconcile form, so you can return to that form and check them off there.

Tip: For a quick list of all of your missing checks, choose Reports > Other Reports > Missing Checks. After you select a checking account, you'll see a report listing all the checks you've written and the missing numbers will be identified.

Reconciling from an Online Statement

If you have an online bank account, you can download a current statement and then sit back while QuickBooks tries to reconcile it with the account's register.

1. Choose Online > Online Banking > Online Banking Center.

2. Click the Send button to send transactions and receive statements. The information will be transferred and the latest QuickStatements for your accounts will appear in the Received Items list.

3. Select the QuickStatement for the account in the Received Items list and click the View button. QuickBooks will open the statement and automatically attempt to reconcile it against payment transactions you have recorded. When it's done, you'll see a message indicating whether or not all the bank transactions matched ones in your checking account register (see Figure 7.23).

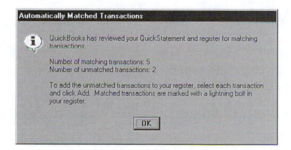

Fig 7.23 After QuickBooks tries to reconcile your register with an online account statement, this message tells you about unmatched transactions.

4. Click the OK button to put the message away so you can see the Match QuickStatement window shown in Figure 7.24.

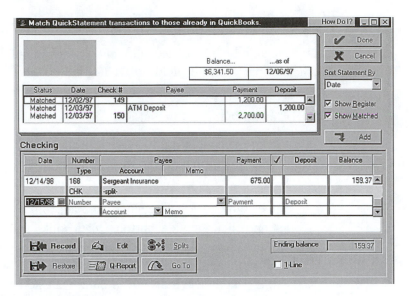

Figure 7.24 The Match QuickStatement window.

5.   Scroll the list of transactions at the top until you see one with the status Unmatched.

6.   Select the unmatched transaction and click the Add button to add it to your bank account register below.

7.   Repeat steps 5 and 6 until you've matched all the transactions.

8.   Click the Done button to close the Match QuickStatement window.

USING REPORTS AND GRAPHS

Most of your time using QuickBooks will be spent filling in one form after another to capture your accounting data in individual transactions. But when it comes time to review or analyze your company's financial activity, you will need to see more than one transaction at a time. Account registers will show you the past activity for a particular customer or in your checking account, for example, but you need a report or a graph to display or print data from a group of accounts or customers.

You can produce reports and graphs on any selection of your Quick-Books data, but typically you'll use them to view your business's activity on a weekly, monthly, quarterly, or annual basis. Once you have a report or graph on the screen, you can zoom in to examine the details of specific invoices or other transactions.

Using QuickReports

QuickReports are lists of transactions about a certain vendor, customer, item, employee, or account. What you see in the QuickReport depends on the source from which you're making it:

- If you select an expense account, you'll see all the year-to-date transactions for that account.

- If you select a customer or job, you'll see all the unpaid invoices and payments that have not been applied for that customer or job.

- If you select a billable item, you'll see all the invoices, purchase orders, and item receipts for the current year that include that item.

- If you select a transaction in a register, the report shows all the year-to-date transactions for that employee, customer or vendor.

The QuickReport shown in Figure 8.1 was made from one item in the checking account register. It shows every paycheck to this employee in chronological order, plus the total amount.

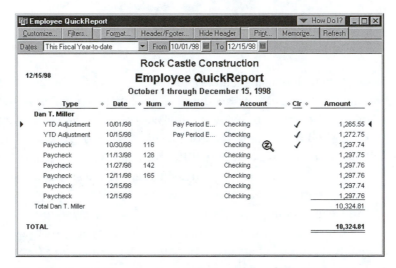

Figure 8.1 QuickReports are an easy way to see a list of transactions for a single account, customer, vendor, or employee.

 Note: *The formatting and filtering buttons at the top of the Quick-Report window are the same ones in regular reports.*

You can make a QuickReport about any item on any QuickBooks list, or from any account or customer register.

QuickReports from Lists

To produce a QuickReport for an item on a list:

1. Choose the list name from the Lists menu.

2. Click on the item you want to select it.

3. Press Ctrl-Q or choose the QuickReport command with the Reports menu button at the bottom of the list window. You'll see the report window shown in Figure 8.2.

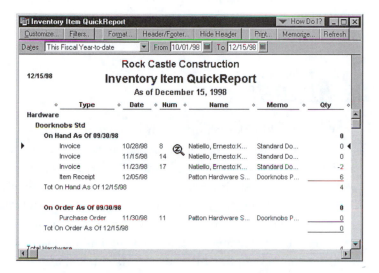

Figure 8.2 When you make a QuickReport for an inventory item, you'll see all the invoices, receipts, and purchase orders that include that item.

Because this is a report for an item, you see item receipts and invoices that include this item, and also purchase orders and a count of items on hand.

QuickReports from Registers

QuickBooks makes a transaction register for each customer and account you have, and you can make a QuickReport directly from these registers.

1. Choose Lists > Chart of Accounts or Lists > Customers:Jobs to display the appropriate list window.

2. Click on the account or customer:job on which you want a report.

3. Press Ctrl-R, or choose the Use Register command with the Activities menu button. You'll see the register for that account.

4. Press Ctrl-Q or click the QReport button at the bottom of the register window.

Zooming into a QuickReport

Notice the magnifying glass pointer in the report examples. You can use this pointer to select and view more details about any QuickReport. Just double-click an item in the report to see the actual form you filled out for that transaction. You can also double-click a total or subtotal in a report to see more details about the transactions that make up that total.

Using Reports

With QuickBooks reports, you can view or print virtually any of your accounting records in dozens of easy-to-read formats. Reports usually show more detail than QuickReports. For example, an accounts receivable QuickReport lists invoices you've created in chronological order, while the A/R reports on the Reports menu can show which customers owe you money and how long they've owed it to you, your collections history, or invoicing and payment details on an individual customer. The Reports menu offers more than 100 different reports you can use to analyze your data. See "About the Reports," later in this chapter, for information about how you might use each type of report.

You can customize any report to change the reporting period, the selection of accounts or customers, the level of detail, and other factors that affect what data you're viewing and how it is displayed.

Opening a Report

To open a report, choose one of the report names from the Reports menu. You'll see the report window shown in Figure 8.3.

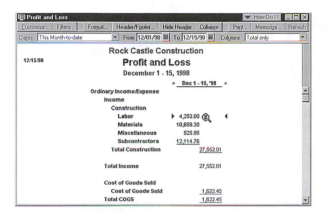

Figure 8.3 This Profit and Loss report is one of more than 100 predefined reports in QuickBooks.

Each report covers a specific period of time. Depending on the type of report you choose, it may show activity from the current day, week, month, quarter, or fiscal year. Reports can also show activity for a future period if you have set up a budget. (See "budgets" in the Help system index for more information.)

Customizing a Report

Along with the data, the report window includes controls and data boxes you can use to customize the report. You can also create a report essentially from scratch by choosing Reports > Custom Reports, but it's much easier to choose a report that's close to what you want and then modify it slightly than it is to build a report from scratch. Let's look at the options in detail.

Choosing the Reporting Period

The Dates, From, and To boxes at the top of the report window let you select a time period for the report to cover. Just choose an option from the Dates pop-up list (see Figure 8.4), and the From and To dates change automatically to cover that period. The specific options you have depend on which report you're looking at, but there are always lots of choices.

Figure 8.4 The Dates pop-up list.

If you want a reporting period that's different from any of the options shown on the Dates list, just select and edit the dates in the From and To boxes then click the Refresh button in the upper-right corner of the report window to update the report.

Tip: **When you change the dates in the From and To boxes, the pop-up list selection automatically changes to Custom. The dates you entered are stored as the Custom reporting period. You can use them again in the future by choosing the Custom command from the bottom of the Dates list.**

Adding Detail Columns

The Columns pop-up list (see Figure 8.5) shows you how data is summarized in the report.

Figure 8.5 The Columns pop-up list.

Many reports are typically displayed with the Total Only option selected, so you'll see one set of columns for the entire reporting period. However, you can choose other options from the Columns pop-up list to show a separate group of columns for each day or week during the reporting period. You can also break out data in certain reports by employee, vendor, customer, item, class, or other designations. Check out the Columns pop-up list in each report you display to see options for that particular report.

 Note: *When you add groups of columns to a report, they are added to the right side of the report, and you must scroll to the right to see them.*

Using the Customize Options

The Customize button allows you to select which data columns are shown for each report. Unlike the Columns pop-up list (which simply adds groups of columns for more detail), the Customize button lets you add or delete columns that present additional types of data.

When you click the Customize button, you'll see the Customize Report dialog box shown in Figure 8.6.

Figure 8.6 You can use the Customize Report dialog box to show or hide report columns.

Different reports have different customizing options, but this example shows the types of choices available. By checking or unchecking the checkboxes, you can add or remove columns of information in the report.

You can also use this dialog box to:

- Change the reporting period (see "Choosing the Reporting Period," earlier in this chapter).

- Add other sets of columns for more detail (see the previous section).

- Choose either the Cash or Accrual method for compiling the data (see "Cash versus Accrual," in Chapter 4).

Finally, you can click the Advanced button to hide rows or columns that have zero balances or that don't show any activity for the current reporting period, or to change the reporting "year" used in the report.

The Filters buttons in the Customize Report dialog box lets you apply data filters, a topic that we'll cover next.

Filtering Data in a Report

Each report has a default data filter, or a way of selecting the data it displays. But you can further refine the data selection or choose a totally different selection with the Filters button at the top of the report window or inside the Customize Report dialog box. When you click the Filters button, you'll see the Report Filters dialog box shown in Figure 8.7.

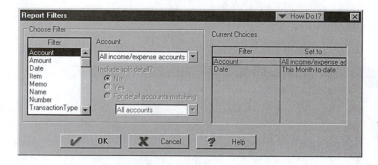

Figure 8.7
Use the Report Filters dialog box to change the selection of data in a report.

The current filter choices are shown in the list at the right. You can modify these or add other filters to create alternate selections of data. For example, you can get a report that specifies only a particular customer:job's information with detail of just the subcontractors on the job.

To change the current filter options or add new ones:

1. Select the Filter in the Current Choices box at the right. You'll see the options set for this filter in the Choose Filter area at the left.

2. Reset the filter options by choosing them from pop-up lists, with radio buttons or checkboxes, or by typing matching text or data into an entry box.

3. Choose another filter in the Current Choices box and modify its options, or add a new filter by selecting its name in the Choose Filter list and then setting its options.

4. Click the OK button to apply the filter to the report.

Note: *When you apply a filter, the filter is temporary—that is, the report will revert to its default settings when you display it the next time. To save a set of filter options, you must memorize the report. To store more than one filter for a report, you must memorize the first report, change the filter, and then memorize the second report (see "Memorizing Reports," later in this chapter).*

Building a Report from Scratch

If you really want to do things the hard way, you can build a report from scratch.

1. Choose Reports > Custom Report. You'll see a report window with the Customize Report dialog box on top of it. The report in the window is a standard Profit & Loss report, but the Customize Report dialog box looks like the one shown in Figure 8.8.

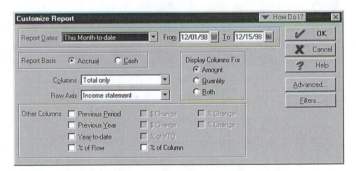

Figure 8.8 When you start with the Custom Report, you can use the Customize Report dialog box to select the way data is organized.

2. Compare this dialog box with the one shown in Figure 8.6. You'll notice that because this is a custom report, there's an extra pop-up list called Row Axis.

3. Choose an option from the Row Axis pop-up list to select the type of data you want reported.

4. Select other options as covered under "Using the Customize Options," earlier in this chapter.

5. Click the OK button to view the report. If it's not what you want, you can always click the Customize button in the report window again and reset the report options.

Formatting a Report

Aside from the selection of data, you can change the look of a report by setting options for how the data or labels in the report are displayed.

 Note: *As with filters, any changes you make to the header, footer, data formats, or fonts used in a report are temporary—that is, they apply only to the report you currently have on the screen. When you display the report again, all the default settings will be restored. To preserve formatting changes so you will see them again in the future, you must memorize the report. See "Memorizing Reports," later in this chapter.*

Formatting Data and Labels

To change the appearance of data or report labels:

1. Click the Format button. You will see a group of formatting options shown in Figure 8.9.

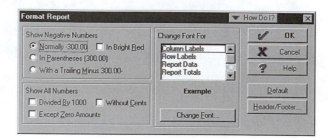

Figure 8.9 The Format Report dialog box.

2. Click the radio buttons or checkboxes at the left to reset numeric display options.

3. Double-click a data category in the list at the right (or select it and then click the Change Font button below). You'll see a dialog box like the one shown in Figure 8.10.

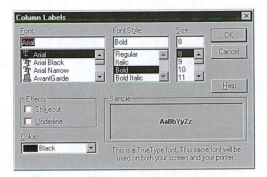

Figure 8.10 You can change the font, size, and style of any text in the report using this dialog box; the dialog box name shows which area of the report you're changing.

4. Choose the font, size, style, type effects, and color options you want, and then click the OK button to apply the changes you made and put away this dialog box.

5. Click the OK button in the Format Report dialog box to reformat the report.

Tip: If you make formatting changes and decide you don't like them, click the Format button and then click the Default button in the Format Report dialog box.

Changing Headers and Footers

QuickBooks includes a header and footer in every report it creates. You can customize this information if you like.

1. Click the Header/Footer button to display the Format Header/Footer dialog box shown in Figure 8.11.

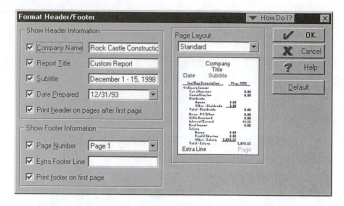

Figure 8.11 The Format Header/Footer dialog box.

2. Choose an option from the Page Layout pop-up menu to change the alignment and position of header and footer data. The page layout preview below shows you how different layouts will look.

3. Click the checkboxes at the left to eliminate portions of the header and footer data, or select the text inside the data boxes and change it to use different text in the title, subtitle, or other areas.

4. Click the OK button to apply the changes.

 Tip: *To hide the header and footer information from the report and make the most of your screen space, click the Hide Header button in the report window.*

Collapsing a Report

Most reports displaying multiple columns have a generous amount of space between each column. This space helps you isolate various pieces of data more easily, but it also hogs space on your screen or on paper. By clicking the Collapse button in the report window, you can collapse a report to display more of its data on your screen or on one piece of paper.

A collapsed report looks like the one shown in Figure 8.12.

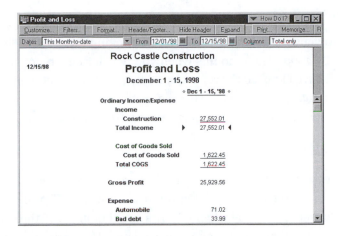

Figure 8.12 You can collapse the columns in a report to remove excess space between them.

Compare this format with Figure 8.3.

Previewing and Printing Reports

To print or preview a report, click the Print button at the top of the report window. You'll see a Print Reports dialog box like the one shown in Figure 8.13.

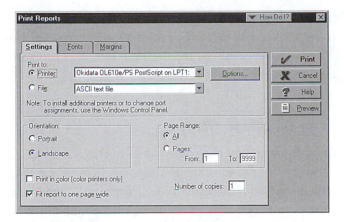

Figure 8.13 The Print Reports dialog box.

This one dialog box lets you change the report's margins with the Margins tab, change the font used for the whole report with the Fonts tab, and set the page range or number of copies. Let's look at three important options that are particularly helpful in providing you with the report printouts you want.

The Preview Button

You can preview the report at any time by clicking the Preview button. It's an especially good idea to do this when you're printing a report for the first time or you have changed the report by adding or deleting columns. The preview screen lets you display each page of the report and zoom in to read details. You can also print the report directly from the preview screen.

Orientation

You can set the Orientation option when you display the Settings tab's options in the Print Reports dialog box (as shown in Figure 8.13). Many QuickBooks reports contain lots of rows and columns. If there are more rows or columns than will fit on one page, QuickBooks automatically adds pages. A printout can be a little confusing when it contains extra pages for both extra columns (pages across) and rows (pages down), so you may want to try choosing the Landscape paper orientation to help with this problem. If a report is only one or two columns wider than a single vertical (portrait) page, you can often squeeze the extra columns onto one page by switching the page orientation from portrait to landscape. Be sure to preview the report before printing to see if this works.

 Tip: *You can also squeeze extra data onto a page by using a smaller font (click the Fonts tab) or by making the margins smaller (click the Margins tab and reset the top, bottom, left, or right margin values). You must set margins of at least 0.25 inch.*

Fit Report to One Page Wide

Another way to fit more data onto one page is to check the Fit Report to One Page Wide box at the bottom of the Settings tab in the Print Reports dialog box. QuickBooks will automatically reduce the size of the font used in the report in a valiant attempt to fit all of the report's columns and rows on one page. If the report is really too large for one page, clicking this option will result in type that's too small to read—and even then it won't work properly. But if your report is only slightly too tall or wide for a page, this is a good option to try. As with other report printing options, it's best to preview the report first to see if it's what you'll want on paper.

Memorizing Reports

After you've displayed a report and have set a lot of custom formatting, filter, or printing options, you may want to save it, or memorize it, for use at a later date. The Memorize button at the top right of the report window lets you do this.

1. Click the Memorize button and you'll see the Memorize Report dialog box shown in Figure 8.14.

Figure 8.14
The Memorize Report dialog box.

When you memorize a report, you give it a unique name using this dialog box. Edit the memorized report name. (QuickBooks will not memorize a report using the same name as a standard report from the Reports menu.)

2. Click the OK button. The report name will be added to the Memorized Report list.

Displaying a Memorized Report

To display a memorized report:

1. Choose Reports > Memorized Reports. You'll see the Memorized Report list shown in Figure 8.15.

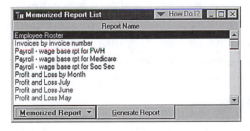

Figure 8.15 The memorized report list.

2. Double-click on the report you want to display. Alternatively, you can select the report name in the list and then click the Generate Report button at the bottom.

Renaming or Deleting a Memorized Report

You can easily change the name of a memorized report or delete it from the Memorized Report list.

1. Choose Reports > Memorized Reports to display the Memorized Report list.

2. Select the report you want to edit or delete.

3. Choose Edit or Delete with the Memorized Report menu button. If you're editing the report name, you'll see a dialog box where you can change it.

4. Click the OK button in the renaming dialog box or the delete confirmation dialog box to rename or delete the report.

About the Reports

Now let's take a brief look at the types of reports you have available in QuickBooks so you'll have an idea about why you would use each of them.

Profit & Loss and Balance Sheet Reports

The first two reports on the Reports menu are the most important because they show a summary of all your business finances. The Profit & Loss report shows whether your business is making a profit, and the Balance Sheet report compares your assets and liabilities. These two reports are often requested when you apply for a loan or mortgage, and they're also the first thing your accountant will ask for. If your accountant needs more information about a particular account on one of the reports, you can return to QuickBooks, display the report, double-click on that line item, and then print out the detail report that shows all the supporting transactions.

A/R Reports

A/R (accounts receivable) reports show you which customers owe you money and how long they've owed it to you. This information is useful when you're considering doing more work for a customer and you need to know the customer's payment history. These reports also help you project future cash flows from receivables. A new Unbilled Costs by Job report lists un-billed expenses for each job on your Customer:Job list.

 Tip: *To see a list of unpaid invoices for a particular customer, choose Lists > Customers:Jobs, select a customer:job name, then press Ctrl-Q.*

Sales Reports

Sales reports show you which goods you've sold by item, customer, or sales representative. You can see which inventory items are moving fastest, which salespeople are selling the most, and which customers prefer which items. For example, you might prepare a weekly sales report that shows which of your salespeople is performing the best.

Purchase Reports

Purchase reports show you, by item or by vendor, what you've spent on goods and services for your business. Sorted by item, the report can help you see quickly what you spend so you can compare quotes offered by prospective vendors against what you've spent in the past. You can also use purchase reports to help you decide whether it might be less expensive to perform some services yourself rather than hire a subcontractor.

Inventory Reports

Inventory reports show you how much stock you have on hand and what it's worth. You may need to increase (or decrease) inventory to cover seasonal fluctuations or adjust your purchasing methods. You may also wish to adjust your pricing to cover increased costs. One of the inventory reports is a price list you can print and use when making changes to your pricing structure. Other reports show your stock sorted by vendor or by item, and you can use these to see how many of each item you have on hand and the average price you paid for them. You can also print out a physical inventory worksheet that lists all the items you carry and has blanks to fill in as you make your physical count.

A/P Reports

A/P (accounts payable) reports show you how much money you owe to your vendors and tax agencies. These can be invaluable in managing your cash flow on a weekly or monthly basis. One report shows your payables by vendor so you can see how much you owe each one as well as the aging—that is, how long you've owed the money. You can also make reports that show your sales tax liability and the amount of money you paid your subcontractors (to whom you send 1099 forms at tax time).

Budget Reports

Budget reports let you compare actual income and expenses with projected income and expenses. To use these, you must set up a budget. For more information, see "budgets" in the Help system index.

Transaction and Transaction Detail Reports

These reports show you all your transactions (bills paid and received, checks written, invoices and purchase orders created, and so on) by date, account, customer, or vendor. These help you view your overall business activity by month or quarter, for example, so you can compare it with previous periods. It's also a quick way to look for a specific transaction if you can't remember when it occurred, because you can view transactions for the year, quarter, or month, or for just a few days.

Payroll Reports

These reports show your payroll expenses by employee, by withholding liability account, or by date. For example, you would use the Liabilities by Item report to see how much you will owe in federal and state withholding tax in a quarter. (See Chapter 9, "Quarterly Activities," for more on this.) In QuickBooks version 6, there are new reports that list all payroll items and payroll transactions.

List Reports

These reports allow you to filter and print phone lists or contact information lists for vendors, employees, and customers. You can also print out lists of accounts (for tax preparation), memorized transactions, payroll items, to-do lists, and discount terms you offer customers.

Project Reports

Project reports are very useful for a quick look at whether or not a job is profitable because they help you cost-analyze your profits on jobs in various ways. If you're tracking time by job, for example, you can see how much time each employee worked for each customer. You can also view each job in detail to see whether (and why) you've made a profit or loss on it.

Other Reports

The Other Reports submenu on the Reports menu has a variety of miscellaneous reports, which are described briefly below.

- **The Cash Flow Forecast report** gives you the ability to look ahead and project what your cash flow will be like, if you've set up a budget.

- **The Income Tax Summary and Income Tax Detail report** shows your expenses totaled by line item (as listed on a federal tax form Schedule C) or by transaction, so you can estimate your total deductions for the quarter or year. (See "Estimated Quarterly Income Tax Payments" in Chapter 9 for more information on this.)

- **The Check Detail, Missing Checks, and Deposit Detail reports** show you checks you've written or deposits you've made, or help you reconcile your checking account by identifying the numbers of missing checks.

- **The General Ledger report** details all the transactions in each of your account registers in one handy (though long) report.

- **The Trial Balance report** is a current snapshot of your business in a balance sheet format.

- **The Journal report** shows all your checking account transactions, in check or transaction number order. The Transaction Journal and Transaction History reports show you the details of a specific transaction once you've displayed the invoice, check, or another form related to that transaction.

- **The Audit Trail report** shows all the transactions you have entered or changed and it shows which changes were made. If you're using QuickBooks Pro, this report also shows the name of the user who last created or modified a transaction. To use this report, you must turn on the Audit Trail preference for transactions. (To do this, choose File > Preferences, click the Accounting icon, then click the Use Audit Trail checkbox.)

Using Graphs

Graphs are essentially snapshots of the data in reports. While you might have trouble spotting a slow-paying customer in a multi-page report, for example, a short bar or a dipping line on a graph can make it clear at a glance. On the other hand, charts don't provide nearly the detail you would see in most reports.

QuickBooks offers graphs for six types of accounting information: your income and expenses, accounts payable, accounts receivable, sales, net worth, and budgeted versus actual expenses.

The Graph Window

To make a graph, just choose its name from the Graphs submenu at the bottom of the Reports menu. You'll see the graph in a window similar to the one shown in Figure 8.16.

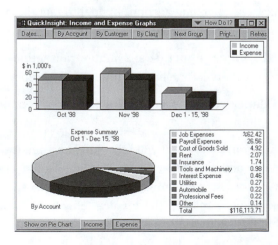

Figure 8.16 A graph that summarizes income and expenses.

Most of the graph types offer both a bar graph and a pie chart view. At the top (and sometimes the bottom) of the window, buttons lets you select the data being charted and perform other operations. The buttons you see will depend on which graph you're viewing.

Changing the Graph's Dates

At the top of the window, the Dates button lets you select a time period that the chart will cover.

1. Click the Dates button to display the Change Graph Dates dialog box shown in Figure 8.17.

Figure 8.17
The Change Graph Dates dialog box.

2. Choose a different preset date option or type in custom From and To dates in the data boxes then click the OK button.

Changing the Graph's Data Groups

The By Account, By Customer, and By Class buttons at the top of the window in Figure 8.16 let you choose how the data is grouped in this graph. Other graphs have similar buttons to change data groupings. Click one of these to select a different grouping.

If you have too many data points to be displayed in one chart (such as too many accounts, customers, or other items), you can click the Next Group button to graph the next group of items. QuickBooks cycles through all the items in the data classification you're graphing and then returns to the first group of items.

If you've chosen an Income and Expense graph, you'll find Income and Expense buttons at the bottom of the window and you can click one to choose which type of data is charted.

Printing a Graph

To print a graph, click the Print button to display the graph printing options shown in Figure 8.18.

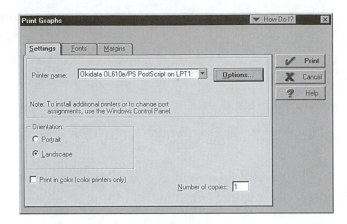

Figure 8.18 The Print Graphs dialog box.

As with the Print Reports dialog box, this one has tabs for general settings, margins, and the fonts used for labels or titles on graphs. (See "Previewing and Printing Reports," earlier in this chapter.) However, you have fewer options when it comes to graphs.

Zooming a Graph

When you move the mouse pointer over bars or pie slices in a graph, it changes to a magnifying glass icon. You can then right-click on the area to see the actual number represented by that bar or pie slice.

To see more details about a bar or pie slice, double-click on it. You'll see a QuickZoom graph (see Figure 8.19) that shows specific expenses, income, or other data.

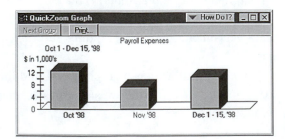

Figure 8.19 A QuickZoom graph.

The QuickZoom graph window also contains Next Group and Print buttons to display other sets of data or print the zoomed graph.

Exploring Reports and Graphs on Your Own

The best way to learn about reports and graphs is to try them out. Choose different types of reports or graphs to see what kinds of information they contain, and then try selecting the options covered above to see how these change the view of your company's data. Don't be afraid to try out any of the options—viewing data in a report has no effect on the data itself.

QUARTERLY ACTIVITIES

If you're making sales and paying employees, you're also collecting or with-holding taxes that must be paid at depressingly regular intervals to various government agencies. By capturing tax-related information, QuickBooks makes it easy to determine how much tax you owe each agency when it comes time to pay up. In most cases QuickBooks not only records and totals your taxes, it also fills out a government-acceptable form for filing them.

In this chapter, we'll look at quarterly reports and payments for sales taxes, payroll taxes, and estimated income taxes.

Sales Tax Reports and Payments

Collecting sales tax, keeping track of it, and paying it to the collection agency has long been one of the great headaches of having a small business. But by capturing your tax data as you make sales, QuickBooks makes it easy to report and pay sales taxes.

When you set up your company, QuickBooks asks you about sales tax agencies and the percentages collected by each. You record the name, address, and tax percentage for each agency. QuickBooks also asks for the taxable status of each of your customers and items for sale as you enter inventory and customer data.

Once you enter this information, QuickBooks sets up a Sales Tax Pay-able account and accumulates money in it each time you make a sale or receive a payment.

Monthly versus Quarterly Tax Payments

Many states and counties collect sales taxes monthly rather than quarterly. In either case, the process of viewing and paying your sales tax liabilities is the same. QuickBooks has a separate Pay Sales Tax activity on the Activities menu that you'll use to handle this chore.

The Sales Tax Payable Account

To see what you owe in the Sales Tax Payable account:

1. Choose Lists > Chart of Accounts to display your chart of accounts.

2. Double-click on the Sales Tax Payable account in the Chart of Accounts list. You'll see the account register shown in Figure 9.1.

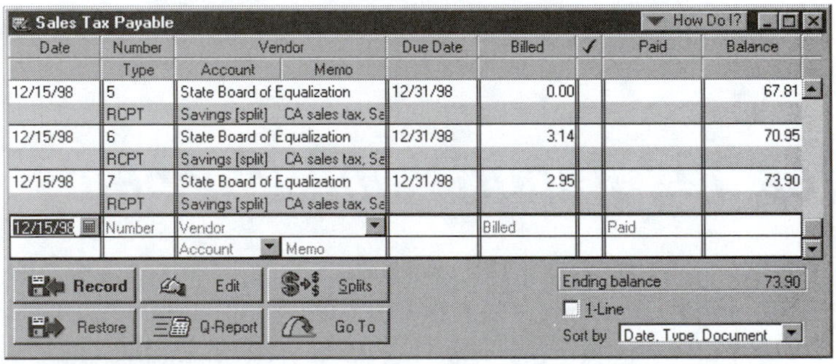

Figure 9.1 The Sales Tax Payable account register.

The individual transactions for which taxes are collected are listed in the register. You can look at each transaction more closely by double-clicking on the line item you want to see or by clicking on the item and clicking the Edit button below. If you want to make a quick entry in this register, just scroll to the blank row at the bottom, enter the data in the appropriate columns, and click the Record button.

For a quick glance at the total sales tax collected for any particular agency, select a transaction with that agency's name in the Vendor column and then click the Q-report button. You'll see a QuickReport like the one shown in Figure 9.2 (this report has been slightly customized in that empty columns have been hidden and other columns have been resized).

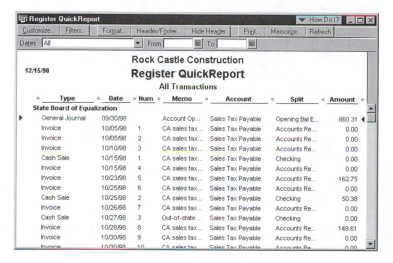

Figure 9.2
A customized QuickReport showing sales tax transactions.

You can use QuickReports to see your total sales tax liability for each agency at any time as well as to check that all the appropriate invoices and sales tax payments to that agency have been recorded. In this example, we're viewing all the sales taxes due and paid to the California State Board of Equalization.

 Note: Many states collect sales taxes for all their counties in one central location. If this is the case for you, it's much easier to keep track of your taxes because you'll have only one vendor listed as the sales tax collector (the state) rather than listing separate vendors for the city, county, and state.

Paying Sales Tax

QuickBooks sets up a special liability account for sales tax payable when you indicate that you pay sales tax in the setup interview. This account accumulates the taxes from your customers, so it's easy to prepare a check when sales taxes are due.

1. Choose Pay Sales Tax from the Activities menu and you'll see the Pay Sales Tax form shown in Figure 9.3.

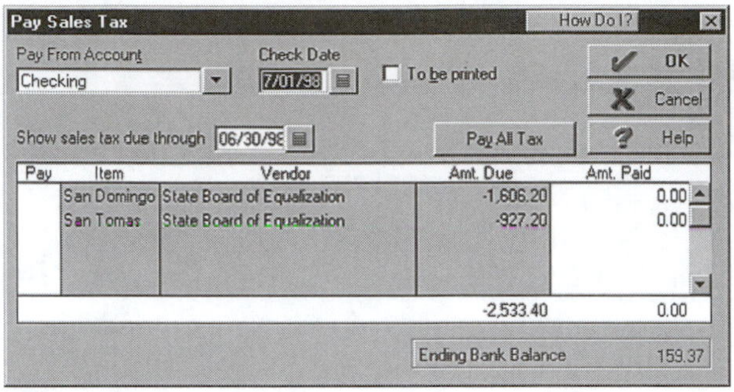

Figure 9.3
The Pay Sales
Tax form.

2. Choose the checking account you'll use to pay the tax with the Pay From Account list in the upper-left corner.

3. Change the Check Date or the Show Sales Tax Due Through date if you like.

In the detail area below, you'll see each of the items related to sales tax that you've accumulated for the quarter. Each tax agency you owe is listed as a separate vendor (it also appears in your Vendors list). The total you owe is in the Amt. Due column.

4. Click the Pay column to select a vendor for payment. A checkmark appears there and QuickBooks enters the amount due in the Amt. Paid column (it assumes you want to pay all of the taxes due).

5. Edit the figure in the Amt. Paid column if you want to make a partial payment to any vendor.

6. Click the OK button to store the payment. QuickBooks will prepare a check payable to the appropriate tax agency (or several checks to several agencies, if there are more than one) and they'll be ready to print. (To print the check(s), choose File > Print Forms > Print Checks.)

Payroll Tax Reports and Payments

Payroll taxes are accumulated in an account of their own, just like sales taxes. You have several options for payroll taxes, however; you may pay them semiweekly, monthly, or quarterly. If you pay semiweekly or monthly, you must determine the tax liability and write a check based on what you owe. If you pay payroll taxes quarterly, you do so through a Form 941. In either case, QuickBooks is a big help.

Viewing Payroll Tax Liabilities

To view your payroll tax liabilities:

1. Choose Lists > Chart of Accounts to display your chart of accounts.

2. Double-click on the Payroll Liabilities account in the Chart of Accounts list. You'll see the Payroll Liabilities register, which looks like Figure 9.4.

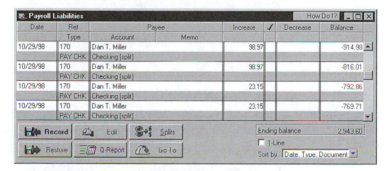

Figure 9.4 The Payroll Liabilities register.

Notice that there are several individual entries for each paycheck you issue. QuickBooks tracks liabilities for medicare, social security, federal withholding, and other items separately because they are each separate line items in your annual tax return. It also tracks any payroll liability payments you make to various government agencies.

In the Figure 9.4, each entry shows "[split]" after it because each of these register entries applies to one check (#170). The double entries show social security and medicare payments where both the employee and employer make matching contributions.

3. Double-click on any of the register entries to see the actual check.

4. Click the Check Detail button on the check form to view the details of items paid for in that check as shown in Figure 9.5.

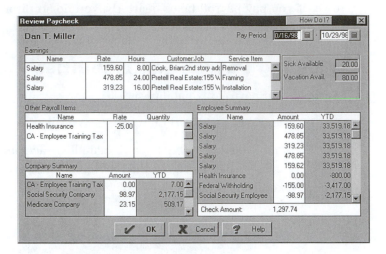

Figure 9.5 Details of a payroll check.

Note: *You may have an arrangement with your bank to take care of your tax payments to several government agencies. Even if this is so, QuickBooks still keeps track of the tax liabilities by the vendor to which they're due, but you simply write a check for the total liability to your bank. With this arrangement, you also set up the bank itself as a vendor to which you pay your payroll taxes.*

Paying Semiweekly or Monthly Payroll Taxes

If you pay semiweekly or monthly payroll taxes, you can determine how much you owe with the YTD Liabilities payroll report and then just write a check to each appropriate agency. The transactions will be recorded in your Payroll Liabilities account register as decreases in the account balance because these payments decrease the total amount you owe.

Viewing the Payroll Liabilities Report

To view all your payroll liabilities for a particular period:

1. Choose Reports > Payroll Reports > YTD Liabilities. You'll see a report like the one shown in Figure 9.6.

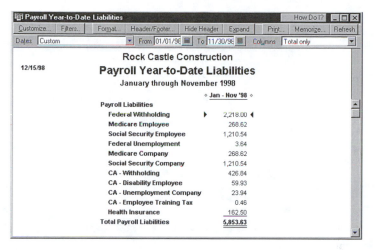

Figure 9.6 The Payroll Year-to-Date Liabilities report.

This report typically shows calendar year-to-date totals, but you can change the dates in the From and To boxes so it shows only your liabilities for the current two-week or month period.

2. Choose a different preset reporting period from the Dates list or enter the specific dates for which you want to view your payroll liabilities in the From and To boxes.

3. Click the Refresh button to update the report if you entered From and To dates manually.

Once you've changed the dates to show the current period's amounts, you can then write checks for each amount to each agency.

Viewing Report Details

You can also zoom into the payroll liabilities report to see how each liability item total (social security, medicare, and so on) was derived. Just point to any amount in the report and double-click. You'll see the transactions that contributed to that total as shown in Figure 9.7.

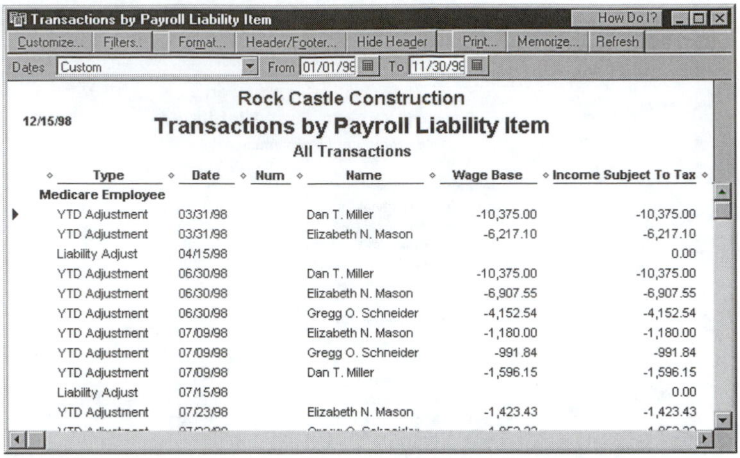
Transactions by Payroll Liability Item

Customize... | Filters... | Format... | Header/Footer... | Hide Header | Print... | Memorize... | Refresh

Dates: Custom | From 01/01/98 | To 11/30/98

Rock Castle Construction

12/15/98

Transactions by Payroll Liability Item

All Transactions

Type	Date	Num	Name	Wage Base	Income Subject To Tax
Medicare Employee					
YTD Adjustment	03/31/98		Dan T. Miller	-10,375.00	-10,375.00
YTD Adjustment	03/31/98		Elizabeth N. Mason	-6,217.10	-6,217.10
Liability Adjust	04/15/98				0.00
YTD Adjustment	06/30/98		Dan T. Miller	-10,375.00	-10,375.00
YTD Adjustment	06/30/98		Elizabeth N. Mason	-6,907.55	-6,907.55
YTD Adjustment	06/30/98		Gregg O. Schneider	-4,152.54	-4,152.54
YTD Adjustment	07/09/98		Elizabeth N. Mason	-1,180.00	-1,180.00
YTD Adjustment	07/09/98		Gregg O. Schneider	-991.84	-991.84
YTD Adjustment	07/09/98		Dan T. Miller	-1,596.15	-1,596.15
Liability Adjust	07/15/98				0.00
YTD Adjustment	07/23/98		Elizabeth N. Mason	-1,423.43	-1,423.43

Figure 9.7 The Transactions by Payroll Liability Item report.

You can zoom another level into this report to see actual checks written—just double-click on the amount of a transaction in the transaction detail report to see the check.

Paying Quarterly Payroll Taxes

To pay your quarterly payroll taxes or report on taxes paid that quarter, you use Form 941, the Employer's Quarterly Federal Tax Return.

Completing Form 941

On Form 941 you report federal income tax withheld, social security tax, and medicare tax. These taxes are based on the total wages and salaries you've paid your employees. If you've been doing your payroll with QuickBooks for the whole quarter for which the taxes are due, QuickBooks already knows your total wages paid, tax payments made during the period, and the taxes you owe, so filling out a 941 form is a snap.

1. Choose Activities > Payroll > Process Form 941. Figure 9.8 displays the first of a series of dialog boxes that you'll see.

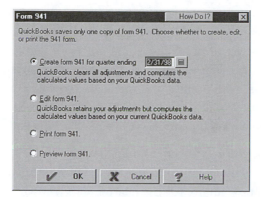

Figure 9.8 When you prepare quarterly payroll taxes, you can make a new Form 941 or edit the existing one.

Here you can create a new Form 941, or edit, print, or preview one you have completed previously.

2. Click one of the radio buttons to choose an option and then click the OK button.

As with the setup interview, QuickBooks guides you through the process of filling out the form so you don't miss anything. For example, if you were creating a new Form 941, the first form would look like the one shown in Figure 9.9.

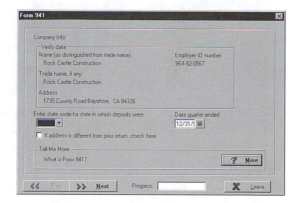

Figure 9.9 You fill out or edit a Form 941 by working through a series of interview screens.

3. Choose options and fill in data blanks on each form you see during this process, clicking the Next button when you're finished. To review previous choices, click the Prev button. If you want more information about the process, click the More button.

As you go along, QuickBooks suggests employee numbers and other information it can glean from your QuickBooks data file. After you verify or enter the total number of employees paid during the quarter, you'll see a series of screens that show your totals for wages, withholding tax, medicare, social security, earned income credits, and any tax payments (called deposits here) you may have made during the quarter. Change or accept these totals as you go.

Once you've viewed or edited your payroll tax data, QuickBooks compares the tax deposits you've made during the quarter with your total tax liability for the quarter, and you will learn whether you've made an overpayment, you owe more money, or you're all paid up.

 Note: *If you make tax deposits semiweekly, you must also complete Schedule B, which unfortunately isn't supplied in QuickBooks.*

At the end of the process, you will see the screen shown in Figure 9.10.

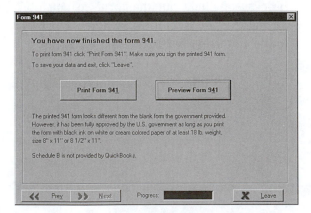

Figure 9.10
When your Form 941 data is complete, you can print or preview the form.

4.   Click the Leave button to save the completed form or click the Print Form 941 button to print the form and save it at the same time.

After you print Form 941, don't forget to mail it (with a check, if necessary) to the appropriate government address, which will be set up as a separate vendor on your Vendor list at the time you set up your payroll.

You can view your completed Form 941 and then edit or print it at any time by again choosing Activities > Payroll > Process Form 941.

Estimated Quarterly Income Tax Payments

Many businesses make estimated quarterly income tax payments. These are usually based on the taxes you paid the previous year. When you have your annual taxes prepared, your accountant suggests estimated quarterly payments for the coming year and he or she may even supply you with preprinted estimate forms (Form 1040-ES) for sending in your quarterly checks.

Business conditions, however, may change the amount of estimated tax you feel you owe during a given quarter. If business is worse than last year, for example, your estimated quarterly tax should be less. QuickBooks helps you compare your tax-related income and expenses in the current quarter with those of the previous quarter. Based on advice from your accountant, you can then adjust your quarterly estimated tax payment.

How Taxable Income and Expenses Are Stored

One of the early questions you answer during the setup interview is about the type of tax form you file. The answer you give tells QuickBooks to track your taxes accordingly, depending on whether your business is a corporation, a partnership, or a sole proprietorship. For example, if you choose Form 1040 as the kind of tax form you file during the setup interview, QuickBooks sets up your chart of accounts so it contains accounts that match the data entries needed for this form.

Viewing and Editing Taxable Income and Expenses

Suppose you operate a sole proprietorship and during the setup interview you told QuickBooks that you use a Form 1040 to file your taxes. Because you selected a Form 1040, QuickBooks automatically set up a group of accounts that can be transferred to a Schedule C (Profit or Loss from Business) form, which is filed with the 1040 form. (For more information, see "income taxes" in the Help system index.)

To view your quarterly income tax-related income and expenses, choose Reports > Other Reports > Income Tax Summary. You'll see a summary report that looks like the one shown in Figure 9.11.

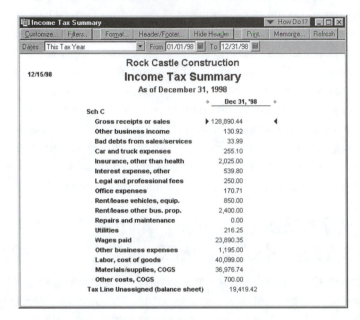

Figure 9.11
An Income Tax Summary report.

What about Tax Line Unassigned Items?

Your Income Tax Summary report may contain a category called Tax Line Unassigned items for unassigned income or expenses, like the one shown at the bottom of the example in Figure 9.11. This means these items weren't assigned to expense or income accounts when they were originally entered, or that the transactions are posted to balance sheet accounts such as assets, liabilities, and equities (since these usually aren't tax related). To avoid confusion later, edit any unassigned transactions that are tax-related now and assign them tax form designations (like Schedule C: Office Supplies). See "Viewing and Correcting Transactions" for details.

As you have written checks, paid bills, and received payments, you have assigned each transaction to one of these accounts, and QuickBooks now displays the totals here in this report. But this report shows year-to-date totals for your tax-related income and expenses, rather than those just for the current quarter. To see this quarter's totals, choose This Tax Quarter from the Dates pop-up list in the upper-left corner of the report window.

HELP FROM YOUR ACCOUNTANT

The first time you make a quarterly estimated payment, we suggest you check with your accountant to make sure you have the proper expense and income accounts for your business. Print a copy of the Income Tax Summary report, show it to your accountant, and ask for advice about adding or changing account categories. (If your accountant uses QuickBooks, you can simply make a copy of your file.) For example, you may want to break up accounts with large balances into a group of smaller accounts.

While you're reviewing your account categories, ask your accountant to compare your quarter's income and expenses with those from the same quarter in the previous year, so the two of you can decide whether to adjust your quarterly tax payment.

Viewing and Correcting Transactions

To see a list of the individual transactions that make up each account total in the Income Tax Summary report, double-click on the amount in the category you want to view. You'll see a list of transactions that contribute to the total.

For example, if we double-clicked on the Utilities expenses total shown in Figure 9.11 above, we would see a transaction detail like the one in Figure 9.12. (Some columns in this sample report have been eliminated or resized to show the totals at the right.)

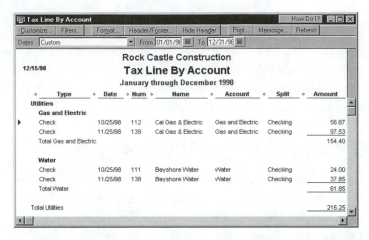

Figure 9.12
The Tax Line By
Account report.

If any transactions are assigned to the wrong accounts, or if you see
"Unclassified" or "Other" in a report, it means that a line item hasn't been
assigned correctly to an account. You should edit the offending line item
and correct its account information before finalizing your report. To edit a
line item:

1. Double-click on the transaction you want to change in the detail
    report. You'll see the original form (the check, sales receipt, or in-
    voice, for example) for that transaction.

2. Edit the expense or income item account in the check, sales receipt,
    or invoice form.

3. Click OK to store the changes to the form. The Income Tax Sum-
    mary and tax line item detail reports will automatically show the
    correction.

 Note: *If the report window is already open, click the Refresh button
to update it with new data.*

YEAR-END AND TAX-TIME ACTIVITIES

By the end of your first fiscal year with QuickBooks, you've probably spent at least a few months faithfully entering your accounting transactions. Now it's time to reap one of the most important benefits of your patient efforts: a series of reports that will remove the drudgery from preparing your annual income tax returns.

In this chapter, we'll talk about the reports you'll use to assist your accountant (or yourself) in preparing your tax returns. We'll also cover some other year-end activities that will put this year on ice so you're ready to begin anew.

Preparing for the Year's End

QuickBooks relies on data you've entered and options you've chosen to sort your transactions into the proper tax-related categories. Of course, if you haven't chosen the right options or haven't assigned transactions to the proper accounts, your end-of-year reports won't be very helpful.

Before you start closing out a year, plan a meeting with your accountant to clear up any questions about how expenses and income have been coded and to plan your strategy for the year.

Making an Accountant's Review File

If your accountant uses QuickBooks, the best way to conduct a year-end review is to create an Accountant's Review copy of your QuickBooks data file. To do this:

1. Choose File > Accountant's Review > Create Accountant's Copy. QuickBooks will tell you that it must close all other windows you have open in the program.

2. Click the OK button. You'll see a File Save dialog box where you can name and save the review file.

3. Name the file, choose a location for it, and then click the Save button. A copy of your data file will be saved in a special review format. (To save a copy of your data on a floppy disk to give to your accountant, choose your floppy disk drive as the storage location, and make sure you have a floppy disk in that drive.)

Your accountant will then be able to open your data file and make any necessary changes. You can then merge those changes into your own copy of the data file. For more information, see "accountant's review copy" in the Help system index.

Verifying Data Classifications

Whether your accountant uses QuickBooks or not, the two of you should review your data and make sure that you've assigned everything to the proper classification. Here are some specifics to check.

Vendor Status

You may have hired consultants, laborers, or other casual workers on a temporary basis. In this case, you'll need to determine whether or not each vendor needs a 1099-MISC form. There's a monetary threshold below which you don't have to file a 1099 for a vendor—ask your accountant what the current threshold is. (For instructions on setting up a vendor as a 1099 recipient, see "Preparing 1099-MISC Forms," later in this chapter.)

Taxable Expense Categories

Unless you've made major changes in your business, your taxable income and expense categories should be roughly comparable to those of the previous year. To find out if they are, print an Income Tax Summary report and review the expense and income categories in it. While you're at it, compare the total amounts in each category with a Schedule C or other detail form from your previous year's tax return, and make a note of any major discrepancy that you can't explain. Clear up any questions about categories and amount discrepancies with your accountant.

Payroll Expenses and Reports

At the end of the year you must prepare a Form 941 for the last quarter's payroll taxes, a Form 1099 for payments to others not on your payroll, and possibly a Form 940 for FUTA (Federal Unemployment Tax Act) reporting. To prepare for this, step through the process of creating each form just for practice to see what kinds of data you'll need for each form.

 Note: *You may already have experience preparing a Form 941 from previous quarters.*

Make a note of any questions you have about the screens you see and ask your accountant about them. It may also help to prepare a Summary by Employee payroll report so you can see the total payroll expenses in each category for each employee.

Cash or Accrual?

Each year-end report can be set to show your expenses and income on a cash or accrual basis. To change this option:

1. Display the report.

2. Click the Customize button in the report window.

3. Choose an option in the dialog box you see, then click the OK button.

 Note: *You should have indicated during the initial setup interview whether you're tracking your activity on a cash or accrual basis. (See the sidebar "Cash versus Accrual" in Chapter 4.) If so, your reports will already be set the same way.*

Tracking Depreciation

If you have fixed asset items (such as equipment) that you have owned for more than a year, they depreciate in value. Most businesses that use accountants are happy to leave the complexities of asset depreciation to them; the rules about depreciation are complex and they change frequently. If you use QuickBooks to track depreciation of your assets, however, the depreciated values will be reflected in your balance sheet each year and you'll have a more accurate picture of your company's worth.

Setting Up a Depreciation Account

To set up an asset for depreciation, you must set up four accounts in your Chart of Accounts list:

- An account for the fixed asset.

- Two subaccounts (one for the asset's original cost and one for its accumulated depreciation).

- A depreciation expense account to store all the depreciation costs you enter for individual fixed assets.

To set up the fixed asset account:

1. Choose Lists > Chart of Accounts to display your chart of accounts.

2. Choose New with the Account menu button at the bottom of the list window. You'll see a New Account form like the one shown in Figure 10.1.

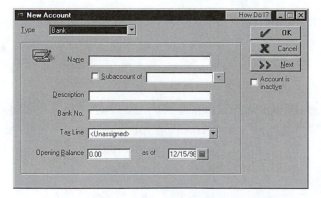

Figure 10.1
Use the New Account form to set up depreciation accounts.

3. Choose the Fixed Asset from the Type list at the top.

4. Enter a name for the account (use the equipment's name so you can easily recognize it in the chart of accounts).

5. Fill out the Description and Note boxes, but leave the Tax Line option set to Unassigned for now.

6. Enter a zero in the Opening Balance blank.

7. Click the OK button to create the account.

Creating a Depreciation Subaccount

If you have several pieces of equipment in one category, such as a fleet of trucks, you may want to use a master account for all the trucks (so you can track the fleet's total depreciation) and then create a subaccount for each truck in the fleet. The basic procedure for creating subaccounts is the same, but you add more information:

1. Choose Fixed Asset as the account type and enter a name for the new subaccount. (Remember to create two subaccounts—Cost and Depreciation—for each truck.)

2. Check the Subaccount Of checkbox, then choose the equipment account you just created as the master account.

3. For the Cost subaccount, enter the price you paid for the equipment in the Opening Balance box, and the date you bought it in the As Of box.

4. Click the OK button to create the account.

Figure 10.2 shows an example of cost and depreciation subaccounts set up for a truck.

Figure 10.2 A chart of accounts showing truck cost and depreciation accounts.

To set up a Depreciation Expense account, follow the same basic procedure above except choose Expense from the Account Type pop-up list, use a zero starting balance, and use today's date as the As Of date.

For details about this, see "accounts to track" under "depreciation" in the Help system index.

Tracking Depreciation

Once you've set up the accounts, ask your accountant for help determining the amount of depreciation for each asset each year and then enter the amount for each fixed asset item into the depreciation expense account's register:

1. Choose Lists > Chart of Accounts.

2. Double-click on the depreciation account for a particular fixed asset to display its transaction register. A new transaction will be started, and today's date will be selected in the Date column for that transaction as shown in Figure 10.3.

Figure 10.3 A new transaction in the Depreciation account register.

Since this account is exclusively for depreciation, you don't really need to enter any payee or type information.

3. Click in the Decrease column and enter the depreciation amount. QuickBooks automatically stores this as a decrease in the item's value.

4. Click the Record button to store the transaction.

For more information, see "transactions" under "depreciation" in the Help system index.

Year-end Tax Reports

Year-end taxes are often one of the most anxiety-ridden aspects of running a small business. QuickBooks reduces the amount of time you spend rounding up tax-related data because you record that data on a daily and weekly basis. It also reduces anxiety because you can see at any point during the year just how you're doing and how much tax you owe. If you pay sales, payroll, inventory, and income tax monthly or quarterly, you'll also have a big head start on paying the final year-end bill.

We cannot, within the scope of this book, guide you through the morass of tax laws, but we can show you how QuickBooks helps you at this time of year. QuickBooks won't do your taxes, but it will prepare W-2 and 1099 forms, year-end payroll tax forms, and a series of reports that will present your tax-related expenses and income in appropriate categories for your tax return. If you prepare your own taxes, the process will go much more quickly and smoothly with QuickBooks. And if you use an accountant, you can either send him or her a copy of your QuickBooks data file to review, or at the very least impress him or her with the way you've organized and presented your data.

Making Year-end Reports

Every report you can make in QuickBooks is available from the Reports menu, as discussed in Chapter 8, "Using Reports and Graphs." The only difference between a year-end report and a daily, weekly, monthly, or quarterly one is the date range you specify for the report.

To make a year-end report, choose the report name from the Reports menu. If necessary, choose either This Fiscal Year or This Tax Year from the Dates pop-up list in the upper-left corner of the report window.

In this section, we'll cover some specific reports you'll use to prepare your taxes, or simply to sum up the health of your business at year's end. As you make each report, print out one or two copies of it so you'll have the data when you're away from your computer. If you do your own taxes, you need only one copy of the report; if you use an accountant or have investors, make copies for each of these parties. Once you file your taxes, keep a printed copy of each report in your files along with copies of your tax return.

Why Do I Need Paper Copies of My Reports?

It's a good idea to have paper copies of reports because you can't guarantee that you'll always have access to the data stored on your computer's disk. Computers change, software changes, hard disks crash, and backup disks deteriorate. In a fit of madness, for example, you may change to a different accounting system in a few years—one that won't read your QuickBooks files. Or, your computer may malfunction in such a way that your hard disk crashes and the computer ruins your backup disks when you try to use them. Safely stored printouts of your vital end-of-year business reports will ensure that you'll have access to your data for a long time, no matter what happens to your computer or software.

The Profit & Loss Report

The Profit & Loss report lists your expenses versus your income for the year; it's a good snapshot of your company's profitability. To make this report, choose Reports > Profit & Loss > Standard. Figure 10.4 shows part of a P&L report.

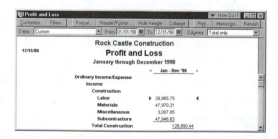

Figure 10.4 A P&L report is a quick snapshot of your company's profitability.

Tip: To see more of a report on the screen, click the Hide Header button.

Your accountant will probably ask to see this report, and even if he or she doesn't, you should make one at the end of each year so you can have a final record of the year's overall activity. You'll also need this report to show to any potential investors if you apply for a business loan in the coming year, or if you are planning to sell your business or a portion of it.

 Tip: *If you use classes, a P&L by Class report gives you precise data on how each class performed for the period.*

The Balance Sheet Report

A balance sheet is another standard way to tell the whole story of your business on one page (see Figure 10.5).

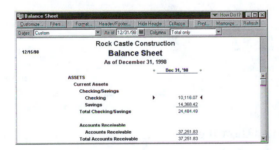

Figure 10.5 A Balance Sheet report shows your total assets and liabilities.

This is the big picture of the total value of your business. Publicly held corporations are required to publish a balance sheet quarterly. You will want to have one at the end of the year as a way to see at a glance how you've performed. This report is also the one you need to show your investors, if you have any, and to show any institution to which you're applying for a loan. In the old days, your accountant would have to do this report for you, but now you can do it yourself by choosing Reports > Balance Sheet > Standard.

As you gain confidence in QuickBooks, you'll find yourself relying less and less on professional accounting help.

The Income Tax Summary Report

The Income Tax Summary report shows category totals of your tax-related expenses and income for the whole year. To make this report, choose Reports > Other Reports > Income Tax Summary. The report will look like the one shown in Figure 10.6.

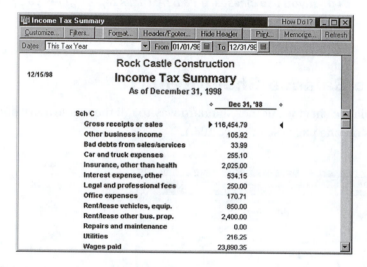

Figure 10.6
An Income Tax Summary report lists your tax-related income and expenses.

This report should show the same expense and income categories you'll need to report on your tax forms.

Once you're satisfied that the accounts reflect your expenses and income correctly, you can transfer the figures directly to your tax form (or into TurboTax for Business, if you use it).

CHANGING REPORT TOTALS

To make a last-minute adjustment to an account total on the Income Tax Summary report:

Double-click on the account total in the report to see a list of transactions that contribute to the total.

1. *Double-click on the amount of the transaction to view or edit it. You'll see the original check, invoice, bill, or other form, and you can change the amount, customer, payee or vendor name, or the account to which it is charged.*

2. *Make the change you want on the transaction form.*

3. *Click OK to store the edited transaction form and put the form away.*

4. *Click the Refresh button in the upper-right corner of the report window. The change will be reflected in the report.*

5. *You can also make general additions or subtractions to an account right in the account register.*

6. *Choose Lists > Chart of Accounts.*

7. *Double-click on the account name in the list to display the account register.*

8. *Add a new transaction to the bottom of the register.*

 Tip: *If you fill out tax forms manually, see "income tax forms" in the Help system index. If you use TurboTax for Business, you can import your QuickBooks data file into that program so it can do your taxes for you—see "TurboTax for Business" in the Help system index.*

The Transaction Detail Report

To back up the totals in the Income Tax Summary report, print out a Transaction Detail report by account and take it with you when you have your taxes done. Choose Reports > Transaction Detail Reports > By Account to make the type of report shown in Figure 10.7.

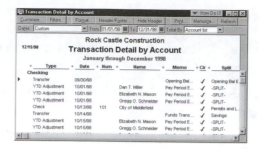

Figure 10.7 A Transaction Detail by Account report.

The report lists all your transactions by account so you can quickly find any particular transaction you've made. Different categories of expenses and income can have different tax consequences, but with this report you can look for transactions that may not have been assigned to the proper account and ask your accountant about them.

The Summary by Employee Report

The Summary by Employee report shows your employee withholding figures and company contributions for the entire year. To make it, choose Reports > Payroll Reports > Employee Earnings. The report looks like the one shown in Figure 10.8.

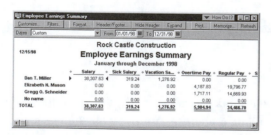

Figure 10.8 The Payroll Summary by Employee report.

The columns show the totals of various payroll items for each employee and for your entire payroll. This report will provide you with a paper copy of all your employee wages and withholdings and your company contributions for the year, and it serves as a cross-check for the data on your W-2 forms (but of course, QuickBooks is using the same data for both).

Employee and Nonemployee Tax Forms

Along with filing tax returns, you must also file forms W-2, W-3, and 1099-MISC to report payments you have made to employees or others. QuickBooks can prepare these forms for you, based on the payroll and expense data you've entered during the year.

Preparing W-2 and W-3 Forms

In addition to figuring your own taxes at year's end, you're required by law to provide all employees with a record of their total earnings and withholding data for the year, and to send copies of these statements to the IRS. You use IRS forms W-2 and W-3 for this.

Creating W-2 Forms

To prepare a W-2 form:

1. Choose Activities > Payroll > Process W-2s. You'll see the Process W-2s form shown in Figure 10.9.

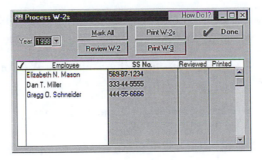

Figure 10.9 The Process W-2s form.

2. Click in the checkmark column to select employees for whom you wish to print W-2s, or click the Mark All button to select them all.

3. Click the Review W-2 button (you can't print W-2s without reviewing them first). You'll see the first page of a W-2 form containing W-2 information for the first employee on the list, as shown in Figure 10.10.

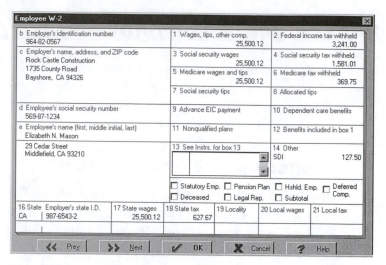

Figure 10.10 The Employee W-2 form.

4. To change any of the amounts, double-click on the amount you want to change. You'll see an Adjustments window where you can change the total amount shown on the W-2 form.

5. Click the Next button to view the next page of the form.

6. Click OK after entering the adjusted amount and the W-2 form preview will show the change.

7. Click OK at the bottom of the Employee W-2 form to complete the review.

8. Once you have reviewed all the W-2 forms, you're returned to the Process W-2s form, and a checkmark is now in the Reviewed column next to each employee's name. To print W-2s from within this form, click the Print W-2s button. You'll be prompted to set up your printer for this form and to load the forms themselves.

PRINTING W-2 AND W-3 FORMS

QuickBooks prints W-2 and W-3 data only, so you must use a preprinted form that has all the appropriate data blanks on it. The normal W-2 forms you get from the IRS are multipart forms intended for typewriters or pin-feed printers. If you use a laser printer, Intuit can provide you with appropriate, single-part W-2 and W-3 forms. There are two forms for each page (one per employee). Print three copies of each form: one to keep for your files, one to send to the IRS, and one to give to the employee.

After the W-2 forms are printed, give the appropriate copies to each employee, keep a copy for yourself, and forward the others to the IRS.

Printing Form W-3

When you've processed all your W-2 forms, you'll need to print a W-3 form, which is a summary of all of your W-2s. If the Process W-2s form is still showing, you can simply load the W-3 form into your printer and click the Print W-3 button. Otherwise, display the Process W-2s form again (Activities > Payroll > Process W-2s) and then print the form.

 Note: *You must submit a W-3 Form along with your W-2s, even if you're submitting only one W-2 for the year.*

Preparing 1099-MISC Forms

The IRS requires you to file a 1099-MISC form for every qualifying person or vendor that you have paid but who isn't on your regular payroll. In order to track 1099 information properly, you must set up QuickBooks to be aware of these payments. You must set up each 1099-MISC recipient as a vendor, then set up the categories for the 1099-MISC form and the item accounts to which 1099-related payments will apply.

Setting Up Vendors for 1099s

If you know from the outset that a particular vendor will receive a 1099-MISC from you (a consultant or subcontractor, perhaps), you can set up that vendor as a 1099 recipient when you add it to your Vendor list. When you do this, payments to the vendor are automatically accumulated in a 1099 account.

To set up a vendor for 1099 reporting:

1. Choose Lists > Vendors.

2. Choose New with the Vendor menu button at the bottom of the Vendor list. You'll see the New Vendor dialog box shown in Figure 10.11.

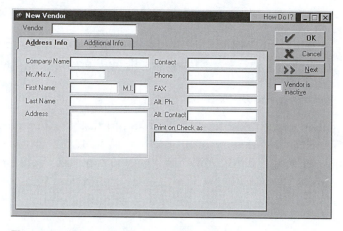

Figure 10.11 The New Vendor dialog box.

3. Enter the vendor name and other information in the Address Info tab.

4. Click the Additional Information tab to display the second set of information blanks.

5. Enter the additional information and be sure to check the Vendor Eligible for 1099 checkbox at the bottom.

6. Click OK to create this vendor account.

If you don't set up a vendor for 1099 reporting at the beginning of the year, you can do it at any time later by editing the Vendor information form:

1. Choose Lists > Vendors.

2. Double-click the vendor whose information you want to edit. The Edit Vendor dialog box will appear (it's the same dialog box shown in Figure 10.11).

3. Click the Additional Info tab to display those options and check the Vendor Eligible for 1099 checkbox at the bottom.

4. Click the OK button to store the change.

Setting Up the 1099-MISC Form

Before you can prepare a 1099, you must tell QuickBooks which accounts and payment thresholds to consider. To set up the 1099-MISC form and accounts:

1. Choose File > Preferences to display the Preferences dialog box.

2. Scroll the list of icons at the left and click the Tax: 1099 icon.

3. Click the Company Preferences tab to display those options. The options look like the ones shown in Figure 10.12.

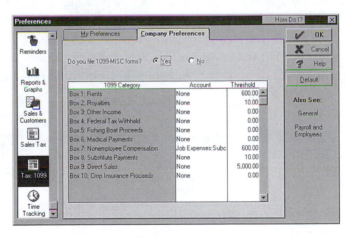

Figure 10.12 The 1099 Preferences dialog box.

As you can see, there are ten different categories of payments you can make and report via form 1099. It's doubtful that you'll need them all.

4. Click the Yes button above the list to tell QuickBooks that you file 1099-MISC forms, if it's not already selected.

5. Click in the Account column next to first 1099 category you'll use then use the pop-up list to select an expense account from your chart of accounts list. For example, a consultant might receive Nonemployee compensation (Category 7) and you might choose Computer Consulting as the account for those payments.

6. Type a threshold amount—the amount below which a 1099-MISC isn't necessary.

7. Repeat steps 5 and 6 for all other 1099 categories you'll use.

8. Click OK to save the changes.

Check with your accountant for the most current rules about who should or shouldn't receive a 1099-MISC and for the threshold amounts you need to set up. For more information, see "1099s" in the Help system index.

Checking 1099 Amounts

You can't preview 1099 forms before printing them, so you should print a 1099 report first to make sure your vendor and amount data is accurate. To do this, choose Reports > A/P Reports > 1099 Report and make sure you've chosen This Calendar Year or This Calendar Year-to-Date from the Dates pop-up list in the report window that appears. The report looks like the one shown in Figure 10.13.

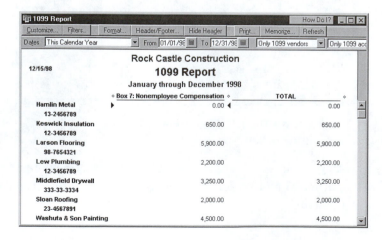

Figure 10.13
Create a 1099 report to preview amounts before printing the 1099 forms themselves.

This report shows all your 1099-related vendors and the amounts you paid them. It will also give their tax ID numbers or remind you that these numbers aren't on file.

 Note: *The 1099 form you submit to the IRS requires a vendor name, address, and federal tax ID number or social security number.*

Removing a 1099 Vendor

If you initially set up a 1099 vendor that you didn't end up paying, you can see that fact in the 1099 report and remove the vendor's name from the list. To do this:

1. Choose Lists > Vendors.

2. Double-click the vendor's name in the Vendor list.

3. Click the Additional Information tab in the Edit Vendor dialog box.

4. Uncheck the Vendor eligible for 1099 box.

5. Click the OK button to store the change.

Printing 1099 Forms

To print 1099 forms for your vendors, choose File > Print Forms > Print 1099s. For more information about making and printing 1099s, see "1099s" in the Help system index.

 Tip: *As with W-2 forms, you can order special preprinted 1099 forms for laser printers from Intuit.*

Preparing Form 940

If your business has employees, you may need to file a Form 940, the Employer's Annual Federal Unemployment Tax Return.

 Note: *Check with your accountant about your filing status for this form.*

QuickBooks can create and print this form for you, and you can edit the amounts on the form if necessary.

Creating a 940 Form

To Create your 940 form:

1. Choose Activities > Payroll > Process Form 940. You'll see the Form 940 window shown in Figure 10.14.

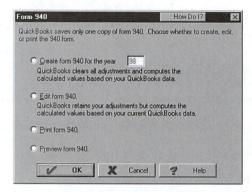

Figure 10.14 When you prepare a Form 940, you can make a new one from scratch or edit the one you previously stored.

2. Click the radio button to create a 940 form for the current tax year (enter the current tax year in the data box if necessary).

3. Click the OK button to continue. You'll see a set of questions and instructions. If you have been making regular payroll tax payments, these payments will be accounted for and will show in the screens that follow.

4. Choose the appropriate options, and click the Next button to continue. If you don't know how to answer questions on some of the screens, see "940s" in the Help system index or consult your accountant.

5. At the end of the process, click the Print or Preview button to print or preview the Form 940. QuickBooks can print this form on plain white paper in a format that's acceptable to the U.S. government.

Closing Out a Year

Many accounting programs ask you to "close out" a year, storing the previous year's data in a separate file and beginning the next year with a clean slate. In QuickBooks, one year continues into the next, adding on to the same data file. The advantage to this is that all your employee, customer, and vendor information is carried over and you can prepare reports that include more than one year's data, allowing for year-to-year comparisons. The disadvantages are that your data file keeps growing larger and larger, and you or one of your employees might inadvertently change a prior year's data.

QuickBooks lets you protect a previous year's data from being changed, however, and it also allows you to compress some of the data in your company file so it doesn't occupy too much space on your hard disk.

Protecting a Previous Year's Data

To protect a previous year's data, set a closing date for it. A closing date "locks" transactions prior to that date to prevent anyone from making any changes to them. Therefore, you can set a closing date of December 31 of the previous year and your data from that year will be safe from inadvertent changes.

Note: *If you're using QuickBooks Pro and you have created passwords for several different users, you'll need to log in with the QuickBooks administrator's password to set or change a closing date. See "Creating User Names and Passwords" in Chapter 5.*

To set a closing date:

1. Choose File > Set Up Users and Passwords > Set Up Users to display the User List dialog box.

2. Click the Closing Date button. You'll see the Set Closing Date dialog box shown in Figure 10.15.

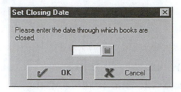

Figure 10.15 Set a closing date to lock out changes to historical data.

3. Enter a closing date or select one by clicking the Calendar icon.

4. Click the OK button to return to the User List dialog box.

5. Click the OK button to close the User List dialog box.

Making a Backup File

Another way to secure a previous year's data is to make a backup file of it. You should do this on January 1 of the new year or on December 31 at the close of business.

1. Choose File > Backup. You'll see a standard Save dialog box.

2. Name a backup copy of the data file and save it on your hard disk.

3. Make a copy of the file on a floppy, Zip, or other removable disk, and then store the copy in a safe place away from your office. This way, you'll always have a file that contains only the previous year's data in case you need it, and the copy will be safely stored away from your computer in case of a fire, burglary, or other disaster that destroys your computer.

Condensing a Data File

If you have thousands of transactions each year or if you should use Quick-Books for several years, your data file will become large and unwieldy at some point. It will take longer to open and close, and reports or other operations will also take longer. To conserve disk space, condense the unused data in your file. For example, if it's June of 1999, you may want to compress the data for 1998.

When QuickBooks condenses a data file, it eliminates the original transaction forms for all activity before a specific date that you set. The transactions remain in the account registers and you can still make changes to the register, but the file is a lot smaller.

Tip: *Don't condense data for periods in which there are still out-standing transactions, such as bills you haven't paid, invoices that haven't been paid, or checks that haven't cleared.*

Before you condense a file, make two backup copies of the file and print a few key reports such as a Profit & Loss statement and a Balance Sheet report. Store these items safely. This way, you'll always be able to restore the complete file if you ever need to view a specific transaction form in the future, and you'll have a printed record of the data you're about to condense.

To condense your data:

1. Close all open QuickBooks windows and choose File > Utilities > Condense Data. You'll see the Condense Data dialog box shown in Figure 10.16.

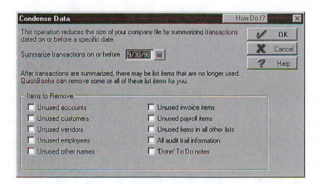

Figure 10.16
Keep your QuickBooks data file lean and mean by condensing older data.

2. Enter a date before which you want your data condensed.

3. Click the checkboxes to select the types of data you want to remove. Along with summarizing transactions, QuickBooks will delete accounts, inventory items, customer records, vendor records, or other types of data that are no longer used (they appear in the data you're condensing, but not in transactions after that).

4. Click the OK button to condense data. QuickBooks will automatically make a backup file of the file so you'll have an uncondensed copy of the data for your records. For more information, see "condensing data" in the Help system index.

Tip: *After you've condensed data in a file, set a closing date to prevent changes to the condensed portion. See "Protecting a Previous Year's Data," earlier in this chapter.*

Onward with QuickBooks

If you've made it to the end of your first year with QuickBooks, you now have a good sense of the program's basics. In this book we have tried to give you a sense of how QuickBooks fits into your business and how to use its main features to keep your finances under control. But we haven't discussed many of the reports, preferences, and dialog box options that you can use to tailor your QuickBooks accounting program more specifically to your liking.

As you move into the second year (and the years after that) with QuickBooks, you can continually improve your accounting system to make it even more convenient and informative. Here are some parting thoughts about how to build on what you've learned so far.

Solve Problems as They Arise

When you don't understand a procedure or an accounting concept, find out the answer as quickly as possible. Collecting accounting transactions is a cumulative process, and what begins as a small misunderstanding can become a major problem if you don't correct it quickly.

Notice Things You Don't Like

When a procedure doesn't work the way you'd like, make a note of it and then look in the Help system index for information about how to change it. Think about how you might add or change accounts or subaccounts to track your finances more accurately. Also, be sure to check Chapter 5, "Customizing and Updating QuickBooks," for ways to customize forms or change preferences for how the program operates.

Work with Your Accountant

Don't be afraid to check with your accountant about any aspect of the system you set up with QuickBooks. If you're lucky enough to have an accountant who uses QuickBooks as well, you'll get lots of specific advice about how to make the program work for your business. But even if your accountant doesn't use QuickBooks, he or she can give you a better understanding of the accounting procedures you need to use for your business so that you can apply the power of QuickBooks in implementing them.

Don't Stop Learning

QuickBooks is a big program and it would take months of diligent, concentrated study for you to learn all there is to know about it. You won't have time for such study, but you should still try to expand your knowledge. Whenever you have a few spare minutes, explore the user's guide, the topics on the How Do I? menus, or the Help system index and read about different aspects of QuickBooks. You may very well discover an easier way to do something you're doing now or find that you can add new enhancements to your accounting system to make it better.

QuickBooks is the finest small business accounting program ever offered, and with your patient effort, you can use it to manage and understand your business finances as well as you know and run your business itself. You are already well on your way.

MULTIUSER FEATURES IN QUICKBOOKS PRO

QuickBooks Pro version 6 allows as many as five different people to use your company file at the same time on a network. Multiuser operation has several advantages:

- You can assign specific accounting tasks such as accounts payable, accounts receivable, payroll, and inventory to different people, and they can all work on the same data file at the same time.

- Each user can set his or her own preferences for working with QuickBooks (see "Setting Preferences" in Chapter 5).

- You can restrict each user's access to portions of the program (see "Creating User Names and Passwords" in Chapter 5).

- If you use the QuickBooks Audit Trail feature, you can create an audit trail that shows exactly which user made changes to each transaction and report (see "Other Reports" in Chapter 8).

To use QuickBooks Pro with multiple users, you must set up the program for use on a network and create individual user names and passwords. This appendix summarizes the setup process and explains how QuickBooks operates in multiuser mode.

Setting up Multiuser QuickBooks Pro

You can set up QuickBooks Pro for use by many different users in two ways. You can use just one computer and allow different levels of access to your data by assigning a series of user names and passwords, or you can set up the program for use by different users with different PCs on a network.

Setting Up Multiple Users on One Computer

Setting up QuickBooks Pro for use by many people on the same computer is a snap. Just create a series of user names and passwords, then turn on the program's multiuser mode.

To learn about creating users and passwords, see "Creating User Names and Passwords" in Chapter 5.

To switch from single-user to multiuser mode, choose File > Switch to Multi-user Mode. QuickBooks will temporarily close the company file (if it's open) and then reopen it in Multi-user mode.

Setting Up Multiple Users on a Network

To set up QuickBooks Pro for multiple users on a network, you must be using either Windows 95 (or later) or Windows NT 4.0 (or later) networking software, and you'll need a separate copy of the program for each user. You can buy five-user packs of QuickBooks Pro at a substantial discount.

Here's an overview of the process for installing the whole system. For details, check the multiuser installation instructions that came with your copy of QuickBooks Pro.

1. Install the program and create your company data file on a network server. You must have administrator privileges to do this on a Windows NT network and each user must have read/write access to that server. Ask your network administrator to handle this if you're not sure what to do.

2. Create a user name and password for each user.

3. Choose File > Switch to Multi-user Mode. QuickBooks will temporarily close the company file (if it's open) and then reopen it in Multi-user mode.

 Note: *You must be running QuickBooks Pro in single-user mode to add or delete users or to change privileges for existing users.*

4. Install each user's copy of QuickBooks Pro on his or her computer.

5. Have each user open the company data file from the network server and log in with his or her name and password. (Once users open the file from the network server the first time, QuickBooks Pro will remember its location and automatically open it in the future.)

Multiuser Operations

With QuickBooks Pro, several different network users can view the same information in the company data file at the same time. However, like all multiuser programs, QuickBooks allows only one user at a time to enter or change data in any particular transaction. As soon as one user begins entering or changing data on a form, that transaction is locked so that other users can't change it at the same time.

To illustrate this feature, let's assume two users (Sara and Ed) are viewing the same invoice and Sara needs to change some information on it. Here's what happens.

As Sara begins editing the invoice, QuickBooks Pro displays a notice on Ed's screen that Sara is editing the data. This lets Ed know that he can't change the form or enter data into it at the same time.

Once Sara finishes editing the form and clicks the OK button, Ed will see a notice that the data has changed, and QuickBooks will automatically update his copy of the invoice to reflect Sara's changes.

By clicking the OK button to store her changes in the invoice form, Sara relinquishes control of that particular transaction, and it is now available for Ed or another user to edit.

✳ **Note:** *QuickBooks Pro locks only specific transactions during editing. It's perfectly possible for one user to edit one invoice while another user creates a new one.*

Managing Multiple Users

QuickBooks Pro has several features that allow you to set up and manage users.

The QuickBooks Administrator

When you install QuickBooks Pro on a network server, (or when you first switch to Multi-user mode and try to create new users on a single computer), you're asked to enter an administrator password. The QuickBooks administrator has unique privileges in a multiuser setup. The administrator is the only user who can:

- Create or delete users and passwords.

- See which users are logged on at a given time.

- Set company preferences.

As the administrator, you can also reserve certain other activities for yourself (such as printing checks or reports or viewing payroll information) by restricting other users' privileges when setting up their names and passwords. (For more information on which activities you can restrict with passwords, see "Creating User Names and Passwords" in Chapter 5.)

User Tracking

If you're the QuickBooks administrator, you can see which users are logged on at any time. Just choose File > Set Up Users and Passwords > Set Up Users, and you'll see the User List dialog box shown in Figure 5.3. Each user name you have created is listed, and users who are logged on are indicated as such.

You can add, delete, or change user names, passwords, or privileges at any time by using the same User List dialog box. See "Viewing, Changing, and Deleting a User's Privileges" in Chapter 5.

User Preferences

Each QuickBooks Pro user can set his or her own preferences for working with the program by logging on, choosing File > Preferences, selecting a Preferences icon, and then choosing options on the My Preferences tab. For more information about this, see "Setting Preferences" in Chapter 5.

CUSTOMIZING QUICKBOOKS FOR YOUR BUSINESS

In the following pages you'll find 20 templates that will help you set up Quick-Books for different types of business. Here are the businesses we cover:

1. Accounting
2. Architecture
3. Art gallery
4. Bed & Breakfast
5. Bicycle shop
6. Catering
7. Cleaning service
8. Computer consulting
9. Construction contracting
10. Crafts production/sales

11. Daycare service
12. Desktop publishing
13. Equipment rentals/sales
14. Farming/ranching
15. Hair salon
16. Landscape design/maintenance
17. Law firm
18. Medical practice
19. Property management
20. Restaurant

We'll offer quick suggestions for setting up your chart of accounts, items list, customers:jobs list, classes, time tracking, and other activities. We'll also direct you to portions of a QuickBooks and Your Industry document for more customization information on many of these businesses.

 Note: *We frequently recommend using classes to track income or expenses in broader categories. You can't use classes to track activity from two different lists in the same file. For example, if you use classes to track customers by type (commercial, residential, and so on), you can't use classes to track vendors by type, or to track expenses and income by type.*

Accounting

Recommended program: QuickBooks Pro

Chart of Accounts

Use the Accounting industry option in the setup interview.

Items

Service items: In the Items list, set up items for each service you provide, such as financial statements, sales tax forms, 1040 forms, and tax planning. For each service, enter a description and the item's cost per unit or rate per hour. Use service items for subcontractors so you can enter the cost and expense item when you pay the subcontractor, and create an income item for each subcontracted service that includes the fee you charge the customer for the service.

Other income items: Sales tax, copying.

Customers

You can set up customer types as classes to track corporate or individual clients, so you can later make reports to show which type generates the most revenue. Use subclasses to track each customer type in more detail.

Jobs

Track projects for each client as separate jobs. For example, for Al Gruen you may do his personal income tax, set up a corporation, and do an audit. Assign each task a separate job. For example, "Al Gruen:income tax 98."

Classes

If you don't use classes to track customer types, you might set up classes to track income and expense by class on your reports. You might also set up classes for owner, partners, or employees to track productivity for each type of worker, or (if you have offices in different locations) assign each office its own class. You can use classes for one purpose only, however, so choose carefully.

Time Tracking

You can track single activities for each job as billable or unbillable and make extensive notes about each activity. If you assign an employee to work on an extensive case, you can use weekly timecards to track the employee's billable hours for each customer and job.

Billing

Use time and costs tracking to fill in your invoices automatically when you bill your clients.

Other activities covered in the QuickBooks and Your Industry document for accountants:

- Billing "retainer" clients
- Using account numbers
- Invoicing for partial hours
- Courtesy discount item
- Tracking write-downs or write-offs
- Customizing invoices for an accounting business
- Tracking time spent on conversations and tasks
- Tracking information about your clients

Architecture

Recommended program: QuickBooks Pro

Chart of Accounts

Use the Architecture Firms option in the setup interview. You can then add other accounts such as Retainer Fees.

Items

Items: Things you charge for, such as architectural services or administrative fees, plus any surcharges or discounts you include on invoices.

Service items: Any specific type of item, such as design development or construction supervision. For example, "Prelim. Drawings" is an item. You can have sub-items such as "Sr. Architect" at a rate of $175, "Jr. Architect" at $75, and "Draftsman" at $35 so you can bill for the number of hours worked by each labor category on preliminary drawings.

Other items: Sales tax, shipping, blueprint copying, and retainers.

Customers

Set up clients as customers. You can track different types of clients by class (such as commercial and residential) to differentiate between them in revenue reports.

Jobs

Track projects for each client as separate jobs. For example, you may design a room addition and a gazebo for Arnold Johns. Each job can be tracked separately. Use sub-jobs to track change orders by adding a colon and sub-job name to the customer job name. For example, if Change Order #1 is the job, then the sub-job name might be Arnold Johns:Gazebo:CO1.

Classes

You might set up classes for owner, partners, or employees to track productivity and revenues of each type of worker, or use them to designate profit centers with subclasses for each employee type. Use classes for one purpose only.

Time Tracking

You can track single activities for each job as billable or unbillable and make extensive notes about each activity. You can use weekly timecards to assign each employee's hours to specific customers and jobs and then call up that information when you invoice the customer.

Writing Proposals

Customize an estimate form to use for proposals. For example, change the title to "Project Budget," change the Item column to "Task" or "Phase," change the Quantity column label to "Hours," and the Cost column to "Rate." Remove the Markup column from the form.

Billing

If you have items that are completed over a long period of time, use the Progress Invoice template to issue partial invoices. If you prepared an estimate or proposal for the job, QuickBooks automatically offers you the option to prepare a progress invoice.

Other activities covered in the QuickBooks and Your Industry document for architects:

- Creating project budgets or estimates
- Adjusting invoice appearance
- Understanding income and profitability with reports
- Tracking time spent on conversations and tasks
- Tracking information about your clients

Art Gallery

Recommended program: QuickBooks

Typically, art galleries are consignment businesses that pay their artists when the artworks are sold. Because you don't pay for the work until it is sold, you don't keep it in your QuickBooks inventory. It's important to have a separate spreadsheet to keep track of the actual works of art in stock at any time, with the retail price and the artist's price for each.

Chart of Accounts

Use the Retail Firms option in the setup interview.

Items

Develop a numbering scheme so you can assign a unique item number to each of your artwork items. For example, "DWP980312" is a number that includes the artist's initials, the year and month, and the number of the piece.

Service items: Appraisals, framing, and restoration.

Inventory items: Framing supplies.

Other items: Sales tax, sales tax group, shipping, discount (to the trade), special discount (for special promotions).

Vendors

Your artists are vendors, but you'll probably send them 1099s at the end of the year. Tracking them as vendors lets you keep a grip on your cost of goods sold. You will need to keep all artist addresses and tax ID numbers so you can send them checks for work sold and issue 1099s.

Customers

Set up clients as customers. You can track different types of clients by class, such as wholesale (for example, decorators) and retail, to differentiate between them in revenue reports. Keep track of important customers and use QuickBooks to print mailing labels for invitations to gallery openings and new artist introductions.

Classes

You might set up classes for owner, partners, or employees to track productivity and sales revenues of each type of worker, or you could use classes to designate profit centers, with subclasses for each profit center's employees. Use classes for one purpose only.

Payroll

Your employees are strictly an overhead expense. Enter your employees' hours into a timesheet every pay period or set them up as salaried workers.

Other activities covered in the QuickBooks and Your Industry document for product sellers not using QuickBooks inventory:

- Entering every sale in QuickBooks
- Entering summaries of sales in QuickBooks
- Issuing purchase orders
- Finding out how your company is doing through reports
- Tracking information about your clients

Bed & Breakfast

Recommended program: QuickBooks

Chart of Accounts

Use the Retail Industry option in the setup interview. Track expenses such as payroll, repairs, maintenance, utilities, linen service, food purchases, and furnishings. Record your income as sales.

Items

Your item list for a bed & breakfast operation is very straightforward. You bill customers for room and board, and possibly a handful of other items such as telephone charges, laundry and dry cleaning, or fax and copying charges.

Other items: Sales tax, discounts for long-term stays, senior discounts, or other special discount rates (such as AAA).

Customers

You won't need to track all your customers with QuickBooks.

Payroll

Have your employees fill out timecards; when you do your payroll, simply fill in their hours in the Create Paychecks form.

Classes

You may want to set up to track income from different sources, such as mail order campaigns, travel magazine ads, or referrals from other sources.

Bicycle Shop

Recommended program: QuickBooks

Chart of Accounts

Use the Retail Industry option in the setup interview.

Items

Service items: Repair, tune-ups, spoke tuning, tire changes.

Non-inventory items: Specific replacement parts for a particular customer's bike.

Inventory items: Frames, wheels, sprockets, chains, spare parts, clothing, accessories.

Other items: Sales tax, shipping, discounts

Customers

Track only important, repeat customers for service or expensive items. If you like, you can use classes and subclasses to track customer types such as professional athletes, mountain bikers, or casual riders. If you don't store data on a lot of specific customers and you want to use classes for another purpose (see "Classes" below), you could create customer:job categories and then list individual customers as sub-jobs beneath them.

Payroll

You can probably use a paper form to track the hours spent on a particular repair, unless you have a very specialized shop with high-end service and products for an elite group of customers. (If so, get QuickBooks Pro and pass along all labor costs to the customer and jobs.) You don't have to use time tracking for your payroll—just enter the number of hours each employee worked into your Create Paychecks form and QuickBooks will create your paychecks.

Classes

You may want to set up classes for owner, partners, or employees to track productivity and sales revenues of each type of worker.

Other activities covered in the QuickBooks and Your Industry document for retail businesses:

- Forgiving charges—courtesy services
- Handling product sales
- Issuing purchase orders
- Finding out how your company is doing through reports
- Setting up custom fields and customizing sales forms

Catering

Recommended program: QuickBooks Pro

A catering business may do the cooking in-house or contract out special food items. You may hire serving staff and bartenders as subcontractors for each job or you may have employees.

Chart of Accounts

Use the Service Company industry option in the setup interview. Add asset accounts for your cooking and serving equipment, vehicles, and dishes, glasses, and cutlery. Add expense accounts for purchases of food and supplies.

Items

Items: Food, liquor, soft drinks, paper supplies, rental equipment.

Service items: Serving help, bartending, delivery, cleanup crew, and subcontractors such as musicians.

Non-inventory items: Champagne, poached salmon, smoked turkey, cheesecake, and fruit trays, for example.

Other items: Sales tax, breakage, markup, deposits, refunds.

Customers

Set up classes to track customer types, such as corporate or individual clients, so you can later make reports that show which type generates the most revenue. Use subclasses to track each customer type in more detail.

Jobs

Track projects for each client as separate jobs. AT&T may hire you to cater a Christmas party and several retirement parties, so use "AT&T:Christmas 98" or "AT&T:Tom Jones Ret."

Classes

If you're not using classes to track customer types, you can use classes for tracking revenue from different employees, or you may have several specific types of parties. For example, you might cater barbecues, crab feeds, teas, and steer roasts. You could use classes to determine the profitability of each type of event.

Payroll

You can simply enter employee time into the payroll, or you can use time tracking if you have employees who are working on several different jobs and you wish to pass along hourly expenses to each client.

Writing Proposals

Use an estimate form for proposals. Enter all the items your client wants for the party, amounts, and prices. Add service items for bartenders, waiters, delivery and cleanup crew, and subtotal. Add a markup for your profit and overhead, plus sales tax. If the customer agrees to the project, you can then turn the estimate into an invoice.

Other activities covered in the QuickBooks and Your Industry document for service businesses:

- Forgiving charges—courtesy services
- Customizing estimates for a service business
- Customizing invoices for a service business
- Tracking information about your clients

Cleaning Service

Recommended program: QuickBooks

Chart of Accounts

Use the Service Company industry option in the setup interview.

Items

Service items: Cleaning fees.

Inventory items: Cleaning supplies such as brooms or dust rags and items you sell to clients such as floor mats or wastebaskets.

Other items: Sales tax, discounts.

Customers

You can set up customer types as classes for different businesses, office types, or geographical areas, so you can later make reports to show which class generates the most revenue. Use subclasses to track each customer type in more detail. You can add fields to the Additional Info tab on the New Customer form to store other specifics about each customer.

Classes

You might set up classes for owner, partners, or employees to track productivity and sales revenues for each type of worker.

Payroll

Typically, a cleaning business will pay employees an hourly wage; you can keep timecards and enter hours worked on the Create Paychecks form.

Writing Bids

Use an estimate form for your bids. If the bid is accepted, you can turn the estimate into an invoice.

Other activities covered in the QuickBooks and Your Industry document for service industries:

- Billing "retainer" clients
- Forgiving charges—courtesy services
- Customizing invoices for a service business
- Handling product sales
- Tracking information about your clients

Computer Consulting

Recommended program: QuickBooks Pro

Chart of Accounts

Use the Consulting Company industry option in the setup interview.

Items

Service items: Consulting fees, computer setup fees, training, research, courtesy discounts.

Non-inventory items: Hardware and software that you buy for specific jobs.

Inventory items: Printer supplies, storage media, cables, memory cards, or other standard parts you frequently use.

Other items: Sales tax, shipping, equipment disposal fees.

Customers

You might want to set up customer classes to track corporate, government, or individual clients so you can later make reports to show which type generates the most revenue. Use subclasses to track each customer type in more detail.

Jobs

Track projects for each client as separate jobs. For Mary Jones, for example, you may consult about a system, install a computer, train her to use a software program, and install memory.

Classes

If you don't track customer types by class, set up classes for owner, partners, or employees to track productivity and sales revenues of each type of worker.

Time Tracking

You can track single activities for each job as billable or unbillable and make extensive notes about each activity.

Writing Proposals

Customize an estimate form to use for proposals. For example, change the form's name to "Proposal" or change the Item column's name to "Service."

Billing

Use time tracking to fill in your invoices automatically when you bill your clients.

Other activities covered in the QuickBooks and Your Industry document for consultants:

- Billing "retainer" clients
- Invoicing partial hours
- Forgiving charges—courtesy services
- Customizing estimates for a consulting business
- Customizing invoices for a consulting business
- Handling product sales
- Tracking time spent on conversations and tasks
- Tracking information about your clients

Construction Contracting

Recommended program: QuickBooks Pro

Construction contracting is very complex, and you must be careful to account for all labor and materials costs so you can accurately invoice for them. Change orders can be troublesome to track and payroll can seem like a nightmare. QuickBooks Pro's time billing and job costing features are a big help for contractors or other businesses that bill time and costs by customer and job.

Chart of Accounts

Use the Construction Company industry option in the setup interview.

Vendors

Your vendors are the suppliers of all raw materials that go into the finished construction, tax agencies for whom you collect sales taxes, government agencies who issue permits, and subcontractors who work on your construction site.

Items

Service items: These are for different services such as concrete prep, framing, and trim; for subcontractors, items such as masonry, plumbing, electrical, and drywall.

Non-inventory items: Items specifically bought for the job, such as lumber, windows, appliances, and cabinetry.

Inventory items: Commonly used parts (such as door hardware, towel racks, and closet systems) that you keep on hand for many jobs.

Other items: Sales tax, freight, subtotal, profit, and overhead.

Customers

Set up classes to track commercial or individual clients so you can later make reports to show which class generates the most revenue. Use subclasses to track each customer type in more detail.

Jobs

Track projects for each client as separate jobs. For Alfred Jones' new addition, the customer:job will be "Alfred Jones:Addition." If you do another job for him later, you can track the two jobs separately. You can also create sub-jobs to track a job's change orders.

Classes

If you don't use classes to track customer types, set up classes to differentiate between new construction and remodels, or residential and commercial clients.

Time Tracking

You can track single activities for each job or you can keep weekly timecards for each of your employees that detail the number of hours per day they worked on each job.

Writing Estimates

Write estimates and turn them into invoices later on if the job is undertaken.

Billing

As you assign materials, subcontract labor, and employee time to individual jobs, QuickBooks keeps track of this in the background. When you invoice your customers, you can call out the time and materials charged to the job and fill in invoices automatically.

Other activities covered in the QuickBooks and Your Industry document for construction contractors:

- Entering change orders
- Tracking time
- Tracking workers' compensation for your employees
- Finding out how your company is doing through reports

Crafts Production/Sales

Recommended program: QuickBooks

Chart of Accounts

Use the Retail option in the setup interview. Your raw material (fabric for quilts, for example) should be coded as cost of goods sold expenses. Use your sales account as the income account for sales of finished goods.

Items

Inventory items: If you enter every sale in QuickBooks, each product you sell should be an inventory part item.

Other items: Sales tax, shipping, discount items such as cash discounts, employee discounts, volume discounts, and trade discounts.

Customers

Track specific customers for mail advertising and special promotions. Otherwise, set up a customer name like "cash sale" so you don't have to track every customer. Examples of customer types might be walk-in, referral, and mail order. If you are required to charge sales tax, be sure that "Customer is taxable" is selected during customer setup.

Jobs

Track projects for each client as separate jobs. If you are selling several different products to each customer, you may wish to track these orders separately as jobs.

Classes

Set up your salespeople as employees. Use classes to break out costs and income for different locations, types of customer, or types of merchandise.

Payroll

You probably won't want to pass labor charges on to your clients, so just enter each employee's hours into the paycheck forms when you do payroll. When you fill out invoices or cash sales, be sure each salesperson's initials are in the Rep field. That way you can track sales by Rep by choosing Reports > Sales Reports > By Rep Summary.

Writing Proposals

Prepare proposals or estimates for your clients by filling in an estimate form that will detail all the items and expenses. You can turn it into an invoice later on.

Other activities covered in the QuickBooks and Your Industry document for product sellers:

- Customizing sales forms
- Customizing invoices for a retail business
- Handling product sales
- Entering each sale in QuickBooks and making deposits
- Entering sales to be paid later
- Recording cash overages or shortages
- Creating a standing order
- Handling customer returns, back orders, and layaways
- Setting up tickler notes
- Entering summaries of sales in QuickBooks
- Issuing purchase orders
- Taking a physical inventory and adjusting quantities

Daycare Service

Recommended program: QuickBooks

Chart of Accounts

Use the Service industry option in the setup interview.

Items

Non-inventory items: Weekly or monthly fees, meals.

Inventory items: Supplies.

Other items: Sales tax if applicable.

Customers

Customer information is very important in this business. You can customize your customer information by adding new fields such as birthdays, special diets, doctors, and medications on the Additional Info tab of the New Customer dialog box.

Payroll

You won't need time tracking; you can simply enter time records directly into the Create Paychecks form.

Billing

You probably bill on a monthly basis. Fill out your invoice form with the customer name and address information, plus items for tuition, supplies, meals, and sales tax if applicable. You can also use billing statements instead of invoices by entering charges directly into your customers' registers as they occur and then printing statements each month. Be sure to establish which method is best for your business and use it consistently.

Desktop Publishing

Recommended program: QuickBooks Pro

Chart of Accounts

Use the Graphic Design and Printing option in the setup interview.

Items

Service items: Graphic design, page layout, illustration, folding, stapling, scanning.

Non-inventory items: Special papers, supplies for specific jobs.

Inventory items: Paper, cover stock.

Other items: Sales tax, shipping.

Customers

You can set up customer classes to track corporate, government, or individual clients, so you can later make reports to show which type generates the most revenue. Use subclasses to track each customer type in more detail.

Jobs

Track individual projects for each client as separate jobs. For the National Watercolor Association, for example, you might print membership applications, show prospectuses, newsletters, notification letters, invitations, painting labels, and award certificates. Give each project a separate customer:job designation.

Classes

If you don't track customer types by class, you may want to set up classes for owner, partners, or employees to track productivity and sales revenues of each type of worker. If you own more than one printing establishment, you could instead use classes to track sales for each place, with subclasses to track each location's employees. Use classes for one purpose only.

Time Tracking

You can track single activities for each job as billable or unbillable and make extensive notes about each activity. You can also use weekly timesheets to track an employee's time on each job.

Writing Proposals

Customize an estimate form to use for proposals. When the job is completed, you can change it into an invoice.

Billing

Use time and costs tracking to fill in your invoices automatically when you bill your clients.

Other activities covered in the QuickBooks and Your Industry document for graphic design and printing:

- Making changes to an estimate
- Billing for graphic design and printing services

- Handling reimbursable expenses

- Adjusting the appearance of estimates and invoices

- Recording depreciation of assets

- Creating budgets

- Handling leases for equipment

- Understanding income and profitability with reports

Equipment Rentals/Sales

Recommended program: QuickBooks

This is for a business that keeps an inventory of equipment it rents or sells to customers. If your rental business entails equipment operators (an excavation service, for example), use QuickBooks Pro so you can track employee time costs by the job; this would be a modified version of the construction contracting business covered above.

Chart of Accounts

Use the Retail option in the setup interview and select the inventory feature. Add asset accounts for your equipment, plus subaccounts for the cost of the item and its accumulated depreciation. Add an expense account for depreciation expenses.

Items

Service items: Delivery, setup, operator labor.

Inventory items: Jackhammer, backhoe, floor sander, sanding disks.

Other income items: Set up your fees for your rentals here, listing each piece or class of equipment and the fee for rental per day or hour.

Other items: Sales tax, shipping, discounts, deposit, damage fees.

Customers

Set up customer classes to track types such as individuals or business clients so you can later make reports to show which type generates the most revenue. Use subclasses to track each customer type in more detail, such as paving contractors, masonry contractors, painters, and so on.

Classes

If you don't track customer types by class, you can set up classes to track productivity and sales revenues of each type of worker (owner, partner, full-time, or part-time, for example). If you own more than one equipment rental establishment, you could instead use classes to track sales for each place with subclasses that track each location's employees. Use classes for one purpose only.

Payroll

Keep track of employee time manually with timecards and enter the hours when you create paychecks.

Writing Bids

Customize an estimate form to use for bids. When the job is completed, you can convert the estimate to an invoice.

Billing

Use cash sales slips for walk-in customers, and statements or invoices for regular customers.

Other activities covered in the QuickBooks and Your Industry document for product sellers using QuickBooks inventory:

- Adjusting the appearance of invoices

- Recording depreciation of assets

- Understanding income and profitability with reports

Farming/Ranching

Recommended program: QuickBooks

QuickBooks can help you track the crops or livestock you sell; income, expenses, and profitability; and short- and long-term loans; as well as help you prepare budgets, do payroll, and get reports. Your farm or ranch is your company; all the separate activities can be handled as enterprises or classes in QuickBooks.

Chart of Accounts

Use the Farming/Ranching Company industry option in the setup interview. Under the Sales income account, delete subaccounts that do not apply. If you use classes to keep different enterprises separate, do not add separate income subaccounts for each enterprise.

Items

Your items are services or products you buy and sell. When you fill out a cash sale slip or an invoice, QuickBooks prints the name of the item (for example, wheat), a description, and the item's cost per unit. Each product you sell should be a separate, non-inventory item. If you raise tomatoes for sale, you might want to have sub-items for Big Girl, Old Flame, Beefsteak, and Roma. Don't enter prices when you set up the items; add them to the sales receipt or invoice as you sell them.

Other items: Sales tax, shipping, discounts.

Customized fields: QuickBooks lets you add custom fields to an item's information form. If you sell many different types of products, you might add a "unit" field to track the type of unit each product is sold in (for example, crates for melons, bushels for corn or wheat).

Customers

Your customers are the people to whom you sell your crops or livestock. You probably won't keep track of all your customers, unless you have large-volume buyers or repeat customers for whom you need to track addresses and other information. For example, if you are a farmer who does some direct sales, you can summarize your sales for the day with a cash sales receipt. Set up a QuickBooks customer called "Direct Sales" and then enter the amount of your sales in the detail area of the daily receipt.

Classes

Ranchers and farmers often operate several different enterprises. For example, a dairy farmer might also sell corn and pumpkins, and raise field corn for ensilage. QuickBooks makes it easy to track these different enterprises to determine the profitability of each. All your enterprises make up your QuickBooks company— your farm or ranch. If you pay for all your seed with one check, you can split the transaction to break out each type of seed and its cost by class so you can track the costs to each enterprise.

Payroll

Enter your employee's hours directly into the Create Paychecks form.

Other activities covered in the QuickBooks and Your Industry document for farmers/ranchers:

- Intermingling personal and business funds
- Customizing sales forms
- Recording sales
- Tracking current and fixed assets
- Tracking long- and short-term loans
- Preparing budgets

- Understanding income and profitability with reports
- Issues for organic farmers

Hair Salon

Recommended program: QuickBooks

If you have room, you can set up a PC and a printer at your reception desk and issue receipts to customers as you collect money for services and products. In most cases, however, you will wait until the end of each day and enter transactions from paper receipts you issued to customers at the time of sale. Track your products for sale as inventory items so you can reorder when your stock gets low. You can use QuickBooks for payroll or, if you rent stations to stylists, to keep track of rental income paid.

Chart of Accounts

Use the Service Business option in the setup interview. You can add income accounts for rents received and sales of products.

Items

Service items: Haircuts, shampoos, manicures, permanents, coloring. Use sub-items for different prices (for example, "Haircut:Child").

Inventory items: Beauty items for retail sale to customers, such as: "Shampoo, Redken." For items that come in more than one size, create sub-items, such as 6 oz, 10 oz, and 24 oz.

Other items: Sales tax, subtotal, special discount.

Customers

Your clients are your customers. It's handy to store client names, phone numbers, and addresses so you'll have them when you need to make schedule changes, notify your customers if you move, or invite them to a special promotion or event.

Classes

You may want to set up classes for owner, partners, or employees to track productivity and sales revenues of each type of worker. If you own more than one establishment, on the other hand, you can use classes to track revenues from each place, and subclasses to track each employee's productivity at each location. Use classes for one purpose only.

Time Tracking

If you have employees, enter time data when you do payroll.

Other relevant activities covered in the QuickBooks and Your Industry document for service businesses:

- Forgiving charges—courtesy services
- Handling product sales

Landscape Design/Maintenance

Recommended program: QuickBooks Pro

Landscape design and maintenance for many customers can be a headache. You have employees and payroll concerns; equipment to buy, maintain, and depreciate; and estimates and invoices to prepare. QuickBooks Pro will handle all your accounting concerns.

Chart of Accounts

Use the Service industry chart of accounts. Set up your equipment with cost and depreciation subaccounts. Set up income accounts for labor, materials, and sub-contractors. Set up expense accounts for repairs, utilities, and insurance.

Items

Service items: Consulting fees, design fees, hauling, planting, mowing, maintenance.

Non-inventory items: Plants, fixtures, materials bought for specific jobs.

Inventory items: Irrigation devices and parts, other items you keep in inventory and sell to customers.

Other items: Sales tax, discounts.

Customers

You can set up customer classes for different types of business or individual clients so you can later make reports to show which type generates the most revenue. Use subclasses to track each customer type in more detail.

Jobs

Track projects for each client as separate jobs. For IBM, for example, you may design the landscape for their new office, install a sprinkler system, and have a mowing contract. This way, you can easily determine your profits on each job.

Classes

If you don't track customer types with classes, you could set up classes for employee types (owner, partners, or employees, for example) to track productivity. Or you may use classes to track different profit centers of your business (design, garden maintenance, weeding, or mowing for example). Use classes for one purpose only.

Time Tracking

You can track single activities for each job as billable or unbillable and make extensive notes about each activity. You can make timecards for your employees that break out hours worked on each job so the customers can be billed for hours worked. When you invoice the customer, you can pull out these costs automatically. When you pay your employees, QuickBooks Pro will enter these hours for you directly when you create paychecks.

Writing Proposals

Customize an estimate form to use for proposals.

Billing

Track time and costs so QuickBooks Pro can automatically fill in your invoices when you bill your clients.

Other activities covered in the QuickBooks and Your Industry document for service businesses:

- Billing for service fees and costs

- Customizing estimates

- Customizing invoices

- Handling product sales

- Understanding income and profitability with reports

Law Firm

Recommended program: QuickBooks Pro

Chart of Accounts

Use the Legal Firm option in the setup interview.

Items

Service items: Research, court date, living trust, word processing. Use sub-items for designating services performed by each attorney in the firm (for example, Living Trust:JL or Living Trust: MC); this method allows you to designate a rate for every service performed by each of the attorneys separately. Alternatively, you can use different rates for the service (for example, Living Trust:Rate 1, Living Trust:Rate 2). Set up items to track services done by subcontractors.

Other items: Copying, printing, mailing.

Customers and Jobs

Set up your clients as customers. You can use names or numbers (for example, client number 187, matter 5 is customer:job number 187:5 in QuickBooks). If you have several cases for a client, set them up as jobs. You can also set up your customers to check for conflicts. See the industry document for Legal Firms.

Classes

You might set up classes for different firm offices, subclasses for partners and associates at each location, or use classes to track income by partner or associate (or by area of specialization, such as trusts or tax law). Use classes for one purpose only.

Time Tracking

You can track single activities for each client and matter as billable or unbillable and make extensive notes about each activity. You can use weekly timecards to track hours worked by each partner for every client and designate the time as billable or unbillable. You can then pass the costs on to the client via invoices or statements.

Advanced Costs

Attorneys may incur reimbursable expenses on behalf of clients. When checks are written or credit card charges incurred, select the customer:job as an expense account in the detail area. When you invoice the client, the costs will appear when you click the Time/Costs button in QuickBooks. These costs can then be transferred to the invoice.

Other activities covered in the QuickBooks and Your Industry document for legal firms:

- Retainers, client monies, and trust accounts
- Billing for legal fees and costs
- Adjusting invoice appearance
- Understanding income and profitability with reports
- Are your contingency cases profitable?
- Conflict checking and other QuickBooks tips for lawyers

Medical Practice

Recommended program: QuickBooks

This category can include businesses such as medical, dental, chiropractic, counseling, physical therapy, optometry, or alternative health practices. Note that QuickBooks does not provide insurance forms or superbills. You can use QuickBooks to handle all your accounting needs, including accounts receivable. If you want to continue using your current system for patient billing, you can still use QuickBooks to track your income and expenses. Choose Help > QuickBooks and Your Industry and open the Health Care Offices document for details on how to set this up.

Chart of Accounts

Use the Medical option in the setup interview.

Items

Service items: Office visits, X-rays, counseling, examinations, tests, procedures. You can use sub-items to categorize different types of procedures (for example, use exams as the parent item and general, vision, or hearing as sub-items). You will probably want to add AMA, ADA, or other numbering codes for each type of procedure or diagnosis.

Inventory items: Supplies, products you sell.

Non-inventory items: Lab work.

Other items: Professional courtesy discounts, sales tax if applicable.

Customers

Your patients are your customers. You can set up custom fields on the Additional Info tab of the New Customer form to track frequency of checkups, birthdays, insurance company, social security number, and so on. You can use customer types to track seniors, insurers, referrals from doctors, referrals from other patients, and those who came to you as a result of an ad. You can add other family members as a new "job" for the same customer (family).

Classes

Set up classes to track revenue by each member of the staff or use classes for different office locations and subclasses for personnel.

Payroll

Your employees are probably salaried; this makes your payroll easy. If you specify each employee's yearly salary and pay interval when you set up employees, the checks are figured automatically when you do your payroll.

Other activities covered in the QuickBooks and Your Industry document for medical practices:

- Customizing and printing statements

- Handling and recording cash receipts

- Receiving payments

- Handling write-offs, adjustments, and bad debt

- Giving discounts

- A/R related reports

Property Management

Recommended program: QuickBooks

Use QuickBooks to handle accounts for your own income-producing properties or those of your clients. If you manage properties for other people only, set up two companies: one for tracking the income and expenses of each client's properties and another for your own income from management fees and overhead expenses.

Chart of Accounts

Use the Property Management option in the setup interview for managing your client's properties. Set up your own business as a service type of business. If you have your own income-producing property and wish to use QuickBooks for that, use property management accounts.

Set up each property as a checking subaccount and as an accounts receivable subaccount so you can track cash and receivables from each property individually.

Vendors

Property owners are vendors because you pay them their share of the proceeds from the property. Your management company is also a vendor because you pay your management company its management fees, lease commissions and maintenance fees, and so on. Other vendors are tax agencies, mortgage lenders, insurance, janitorial and landscaping businesses, and the like. Set up your property owners and your management company as 1099 vendors.

Items

You might charge for common area maintenance fees with subitems such as utilities, weed abatement, and insurance. Other items are rent, repairs and maintenance, and garage rent.

Customers

Set up your tenants as customers because you receive payments from the tenants. You can use types to describe different sets of customers (for example: sublet, tenant, residential manager). You can add customized fields for tenants on the Additional Info tab of the New Customer form, such as employer, salary, credit rating, marital status, pets, children, and smoking.

Classes

Set up a class for each property so you can separately track its income and expenses. Also, set up checking subaccounts and the accounts receivable subaccounts for each property. See the QuickBooks and your Industry document for detailed setup procedures.

Other activities covered in the QuickBooks and Your Industry document for property managers:

- Handling security deposits
- Writing checks for property expenses
- Paying the management company
- Paying the property owners
- Creating property and tenant reports
- Setting up tickler items
- Creating budgets

Restaurant

Recommended program: QuickBooks

As a restaurant owner, you know the importance of keeping accurate records and keeping an eye on your profitability picture. QuickBooks can keep track of your vendors and your income, help you with bill paying and payroll, and make reports.

Chart of Accounts

Use the Retail industry option in the setup interview. Set up a "bank" account and call it "Cash Drawer." Use subaccounts for each cash drawer you have. Use asset accounts for your kitchen equipment and restaurant furnishings, and set up subaccounts for cost and accumulated depreciation.

Items

Items are things that you buy and sell, so you will have non-inventory items for the food and supplies you buy, as well as items to describe the food you sell. You will also have items for sales tax and discounts.

Entering Sales

You don't need to enter every sale; just enter summaries of sales transactions every day or every other day.

Customers

You probably won't want to keep track of your customers unless you have a catering business or a banquet service.

Classes

If you have more than one restaurant, use classes to track the income and expense of each operation.

Payroll

QuickBooks makes payroll easy. Just enter employee hours into your Create Paycheck forms and QuickBooks will create and print your paychecks and keep track of withholding and company contributions.

Other activities covered in the QuickBooks and Your Industry document for product sellers not using QuickBooks inventory:

- Introduction to entering sales in QuickBooks
- Entering every sale in QuickBooks
- Entering summaries of sales in QuickBooks
- Issuing purchase orders
- Finding out how your company is doing through reports

GLOSSARY

If you don't understand some of the technical accounting and software terms used in this book, check the list below for a definition.

940 form   The form on which you report the Federal Unemployment Tax Act (FUTA) your company pays each year.

941 form   The form on which you report quarterly income taxes, medicare, and social security taxes withheld from the payroll checks of your employees.

1040-ES form   The short version of the IRS form 1040 used by many businesses to file yearly income tax returns.

1099-MISC form   The form on which you report to the IRS nonemployee compensation paid to contractors or consultants during a tax year.

account   One category of expenses or income that QuickBooks tracks. See chart of accounts.

accounts payable (A/P)   The group of accounts that tracks expenses you owe or have owed to others.

accounts receivable (A/R)   The group of accounts that tracks money owed to you by customers and others.

accrual basis   An accounting method that includes all bills you owe (but haven't yet paid) and all receivables you are owed (but haven't yet received). See cash basis.

activities   Tasks in QuickBooks, such as writing checks, creating invoices, or receiving payments. Also the name of a QuickBooks menu.

asset   Things that your company owns, including buildings, land, equipment, inventory, investments, and cash.

backup copy   A copy of your QuickBooks (or any other) data file, usually kept in a separate place in case your working file becomes unavailable.

balance sheet   A report that shows the current state of your business by listing all your assets and liabilities. So named because, in this report, the value of assets listed equals the value of liabilities listed, so the two balance each other.

bookmark   A placeholder used in the QuickBooks Help system that marks a specific location in the Help file so you can return to it easily.

cash basis   An accounting method that includes only bills you have paid and receivables that you have actually received. See accrual basis.

chart of accounts   A list of all the accounts you have set up in QuickBooks to track expenses and income in various categories. See account.

class   A group of expenses or income transactions that you want to track, such as expenses related to a certain type of work, or income related to a certain group of customers.

company contributions   Payroll expenses that are paid by your company (rather than by the employee), such as deposits to a retirement account.

conversion date   The date you choose to switch your accounting system over to QuickBooks and begin recording new transactions. See start date.

cost of goods sold (COGS)   The cost of items you maintain in an inventory and sell to others.

credit   An addition to an asset account or a reduction in the balance owed you by a customer.

credit memo   A notice to a customer that you are reducing the customer's balance owed by a specific amount on a specific date, for a specific reason.

current assets   Assets you are likely to spend or sell for cash within one year. See fixed assets.

custom field   A field you add to a QuickBooks form. See field.

debit   A reduction in an asset account.

depreciation   The amount by which a fixed asset is reduced in value over time as a result of wear and tear or simple aging.

desktop   The area of your computer's screen where forms, registers, reports, and dialog boxes appear in QuickBooks.

detail area   A part of a form that lists specific items sold or purchased.

discount   A reduction in the amount of a bill or invoice, usually offered for prompt payment or to volume purchasers.

EasyStep Interview   The interview in QuickBooks that you go through to answer the questions necessary to set up your company's data file.

equity   The net value of an asset or of your company after all loans, bills, and other liabilities are paid off.

expenses   Items you spend money on.

field   A space in a QuickBooks form where you must fill in information, such as a vendor or employee name, or the amount of an invoice or check.

filter   A means of limiting the data shown in a QuickBooks report, usually by specifying only transactions related to a certain account, vendor, or customer.

fiscal year   The one-year period your company uses to track its accounts, if you don't simply use a calendar year. Fiscal years often begin at the start of quarters, such as April 1, July 1, or October 1.

fixed assets   Assets you intend to hold onto (rather than selling or converting them to cash) for more than a year—usually equipment, land, vehicles, and buildings. See current assets.

footer The area at the bottom of a QuickBooks report page that shows the report name, date, page number, or other information about the document.

form A window on the QuickBooks screen where you enter data to complete a transaction, such as writing a check or creating an invoice.

header The area at the top of a QuickBooks report page that shows the report name and date.

Iconbar A strip you can display at the top of the QuickBooks screen that contains icons you can click to perform common activities.

income Money you receive as a result of doing business.

invoice A bill you send to a customer, as opposed to a sales receipt, which you hand the customer when he or she pays for something at your place of business.

Internet An international computer communications network.

item A specific type of good or service you sell or buy, such as an inventory part, sales tax, or bank fees.

liabilities Debts your company owes.

list A collection of certain types of data in QuickBooks. Customer, vendor, item, and employee names are all stored on lists, which are available from the Lists menu.

long-term liability A debt you owe that you do not plan to pay off completely within one year. See short-term liability.

markup item An item you add to an invoice to increase the total price of goods or services on an invoice.

memorized transaction A transaction in QuickBooks that has been stored on the Memorized Transactions list so it can easily be located and recalled from there.

menu bar The strip at the top of the QuickBooks screen that contains menu names.

menu button A button at the bottom of a QuickBooks list window that you can click to display a menu.

non-inventory part An item that you buy or sell that isn't tracked as part of your inventory, such as a piece of equipment you specifically buy for a certain customer but don't normally keep in stock.

owner's capital Money you invest in your business.

owner's draw Earnings from your business that you pay to yourself as non-wage, non-salary income.

payroll deduction A sum deducted from an employee paycheck for a certain purpose, such as federal tax withheld, social security tax, or medicare payments.

payroll item A type of payroll expense, such as wages, salary, or federal tax withheld.

profit/loss statement (P&L) A report that shows your company's total income and expenses for a certain period so you can see whether or not you made money.

purchase order A form you use to order and promise to pay for a product or service.

Quicken Financial Network A location on the World Wide Web where you can get tips, software, news, and other information about using QuickBooks and Quicken.

register A chronological record of transactions you have made in a specific account, such as payments from a certain customer or checks written from a certain account.

reminder   A notice alerting you that it's time to pay a bill, send an invoice, or perform another QuickBooks activity. These notices appear in the Reminders list, which automatically appears whenever you start QuickBooks and you have pending transactions that need to be dealt with.

retained earnings   Any earnings from your company that have not been distributed to an owner or to pay a bill.

right-mouse menu   A menu with form-specific commands on it that pops up when you click anywhere on a form with the right mouse button.

sales receipt   A record of a sales transaction that you typically create and hand to the customer at the point of sale, as opposed to an invoice, which is usually mailed.

service item   An item that describes a certain type of labor or service your company performs, such as writing, carpentry, consulting, or travel time.

setup interview   See EasyStep Interview.

short-term liability   A debt you owe that you intend to pay off within a year. See long-term liability.

split transaction   An income or expense transaction that is divided among two or more accounts. For example, a credit card bill payment might include an item for gasoline (auto fuel) and one for computer paper (office supplies).

start date   The date from which you have recorded all historical transactions in QuickBooks as opposed to the conversion date, which is the date you begin recording new transactions. See conversion date.

subaccount   An account you set up to further divide an account so you can track income or expenses more precisely under the account. For example, utilities could be an account with subaccounts for electricity, water, gas, and telephone.

subcategory   See subaccount.

Subtotal item   A type of item you add to an invoice to produce a subtotal of all the items listed above it.

Syquest drive   A high-density data storage device that uses removable disks or cartridges to store data.

tax ID number   The number that uniquely identifies you or your company for a tax collection agency, such as your social security number or your federal tax ID number, or your state resale tax license number.

Tax Line Unassigned item   An item on the Sales Tax Summary report that isn't assigned to a particular account.

tax tables   State and federal schedules of income and payroll taxes that indicate how much tax you owe for certain levels of income or payroll.

terms   The specifications that govern when payments are due and what discounts, if any, apply for early payments.

transaction   An individual business event recorded in QuickBooks, such as a customer payment received, invoice created, paycheck issued, or bill paid.

voucher check   A type of paper check that contains one actual check per page, along with two receipt stubs—one for the payee and one for your company's records.

W-2 form   The form on which you report the total wages and other payroll items paid for an employee for a year. This form is sent to federal, state, and sometimes local tax agencies.

W-3 form   The form you submit to the IRS with copies of all your employee W-2 forms, summarizing the amounts you have paid.

withholding   Federal taxes you deduct from an employee's paycheck that are paid to the IRS.

World Wide Web   A service on the Internet that allows users to see text and graphics on screen pages at specific locations.

Zip drive   A high-density disk drive that uses removable floppy disks as storage media.

INDEX

P

T